'Falling In Love' After Fifty

...The Best is Yet to Come

Cynthia Wilmot
Marguerite Gauron

Edited by: Nicola Brown
Cover design by: Sanya Dockery
Illustrations by: Marguerite Gauron
Book Design, Layout & Typesetting: Sanya Dockery

Published by: LMH Publishing Limited
Suite 10-11
LOJ Industrial Complex
7 Norman Road
Kingston C.S.O., Jamaica
Tel.: (876) 938-0005; 938-0712
Fax: (876) 759-8752
Email: lmhbookpublishing@cwjamaica.com
Website: www.lmhpublishing.com

Printed in the U. S. A.   ISBN:978-976-8202-57-4

Preface

We lifted our glasses of chilled fruit juice in a toast "to us". We drank to celebrate a friendship of some forty years of tears and laughter, confidences and gossip, chuckles and silent thoughts.

We discussed the lives of other friends, in their fifties, sixties and seventies, who had denied the years and had changed their lives to seek new careers and to discover new loves.

Were these women unusual? Not at all.

More and more women are finding happiness, health and romance at an age when previous generations were relegated to rocking chairs. We wondered; could their secrets be shared?

"Why not?" we asked each other. After all, as award-winning journalists, we had spent many years studying the intricacies of aging and creative living; our work had brought us into contact with a wide circle of interesting women who had shared their philosophies. Why shouldn't we reorganize these thoughts on paper to reach out to women in the so-called "Sunset Years" to suggest how they, too, could experience rejuvenation?

This book is the result... not intended as a hard and fast manual for a rigorous routine but a sharing of some of the secrets we, as "older women", have learned.

Contents

"Are you ready for love?"

Are You Ready For Love?

Frank talk for the World's Most Exciting Women — the foxy fifties, the sensual sixties, the sexy seventies, the ecstatic eighties and knowing nineties – and for younger women who are preparing now for a fabulous future.

Today is a time for falling in love. Whether we fall in love all over again with our present spouses, find new lovers or just fall madly, head-over-heels, in love with life in general, the excitement of new love is here for us to discover and enjoy – and this time around, we have several distinct advantages.

Today we know ourselves; we know what we like, what gives us pleasure, what we want to see and hear, what we want to feel and what we want out of life – and we don't intend to settle for less.

Twenty, thirty or forty years ago we might have had to answer to others; today we do not, we are "us", "ourselves", special individuals with half a century of learning about life and about ourselves behind us. How lucky we are!

Now the dress rehearsal is over and we are ready for the bright lights of centre stage. The big question is, will we bedazzle the critics and win "rave reviews" or will we "bomb out" and disappear into the world of "has-beens" as we enter what could be the best years of our lives, living, laughing and loving. Now we are better equipped than we ever were before to make life great for ourselves and those around us.

Okay, so what's the bottom line? Where do we go from here as we free ourselves from past taboos and the mental and physical ties that have been allowed to inhibit our minds and bodies for so long? And what physical and mental equipment do we have to work with to turn the next fifty years into the best adventure yet?

Over the next few chapters we hope to share some positive ideas on how to polish and refurbish mind and body in preparation for the exciting encounters that lie ahead in that wonderful future that begins today. First of all we must wave goodbye to all the myths and old-wives' tales that have enslaved women of our generations since birth.

Today's women are remaining younger and living longer and finding multiple opportunities for making the future what they want it to be. With modern medical discoveries and increased knowledge of the functions of the human body, our life expectancy could stretch to 130 years, barring disease or accident. For women, the statistics are particularly important. For every year a woman lives today, her life expectancy continues to rise; and women live an average of four years more than men.

Who is going to look after us women in these Golden Years?

That's right, WE are!

So it makes common sense to resolve to be mentally and physically prepared for the years ahead, remembering that many women are cast out on their own in their fifties because of death or divorce. Instead of fearing the future, we must challenge it eagerly, willing ourselves to cast aside old prejudices and misconceptions and prepare for new adventures and financial success. For us, the years ahead can bring not only the satisfaction of a newly-earned independence and self-sufficiency, but the joy of womanhood, including the joys of financial success and rich deep sexual love. Let's forget the calendar – and begin to LIVE!

And to understand the Miraculous Machine that will take us on this exciting journey read on!

YOUR MIRACULOUS MACHINE

Not one of us would buy anything – from a Benz to a blender—without fully reading the instruction manual. Your body is a magnificent machine, so it is important to know how it works and how to operate it efficiently for prime performance and to cut down on repairs.

For most of us, the body runs on automatic. When the sun hits our eyes, the pupils become protectively smaller. When we run, our lungs speed up breathing to pump more oxygen into our blood. If we are hot, evaporating perspiration cools us down and when we're cold; our body creates heat through shiver. What a miracle to take for granted! No need to tell our legs to walk or remind our hearts to keep on beating. This most magnificent of all computers is on the job dispatching orders; "brain to lungs pump faster!", "brain to adrenal glands shoot out some adrenalin in a hurry, danger ahead!", "brain to stomach, produce gastric juices – shipment of fries en route!"

Like any magnificent machine, this one we live in can be damaged. If we insist on smoking tobacco, our lungs will refuse to answer the demand for more oxygen. If we don't create new muscle tissue through exercise, our muscles will grow flabby and weak. And if we eat too much, or too little, or choose the wrong things, even the most efficient digestive tract will go on strike.

Yet even more remarkable, this human machine which can take so much punishment and still stumble along, can, not only repair damaged parts, but can continue to function and we can even stumble along without some of them. God must have had something in mind when he created the appendix, but you can live very well without it.

Scratch the paint on your Benz and it's a trip to the body shop; scratch your finger and new skin appears. Ever try driving with only two wheels? It's much easier to live with only one of your kidneys. Damage the motor of your blender and you have to replace it but your amazing brain has thousands of cells to spare and can function by switching to standby cells after minor destruction.

Your body is sixty percent water, eighteen percent protein, fifteen percent fat and six percent minerals. It runs its own waste disposal system and is even air-conditioned and moisture-controlled.

But begin with the bare bones. There are two hundred and six of them in your skeleton made of calcium, other minerals and collagen. The vital marrow inside the bones is a production complex that produces white blood cells to fight infection.

Your skin does more than keep you from spilling all over; it is a heat and water regulator, a resilient covering which produces new cells when old dead ones flake off. Hair and nails are outgrowths of skin.

Blood – we sensibly call it "life blood" – deserves our complete respect. It carries the oxygen from the air we breathe, distributes the nutrients we consume, collects waste products, and moves on.

The liver is one of our larger organs, a gland which provides the bile to help digestion. (Feel it there, shaped like a big mango just to the right of your lower ribs.) This is a clearing house which monitors the blood provided, taking out the good stuff and sending the rest on. The liver is an auxiliary tank for back-up blood supply. Think of it as a chemical plant, a delivery service and much more. Kidneys come in pairs and filter the blood supply. We can live without one but not without both.

Even more exciting is the nervous system, a vast communication network of small fibres coming mainly from deep in the brain and from the spinal column. This computer system links the whole works together – a two-way information flow to run the body's generation plant, to warn of trouble and to report on damages to this human machine. Step on a tack, and your brain sends pain stabs, via your nerves, warning of danger. Think of pain as a red light at a railway crossing.

One sad fact though is that while your brain has millions of cells more than it will ever use, brain cells, once dead, do not replace themselves. Treat them with respect.

Another remarkable system is that which digests our food. Digestion begins in your mouth which is why Mummy told you to eat slowly and chew well. When your mouth waters, your saliva begins to digest the carbohydrates you eat and allows for smooth swallowing. As you chew, the communication system is on full alert: "stomach, shipment coming down – begin to prepare digestive juices". Digestion continues two to five hours but here is an interesting thought; it's not your stomach which takes nourishment from your food, that's the job of your intestines – yards of muscular, undulating tubes writhing away down there, churning out hormones and enzymes as the food passes along this living assembly line. Finally, when all that's good (or unfortunately bad) for you has been absorbed for use, the garbage goes into the final part of the system to be pushed out through openings Nature has thoughtfully provided.

The bladder is doing a similar disposal job for unwanted liquids. Talk about efficiency and quality control. Wow!

Perhaps the most amazing parts of our bodies are the glands – we blame so many things on them – overweight, for example. ("It's just my glands," says Fat Emma, reaching for the third piece of chocolate cake.)

However, our glands do have an effect on everything that happens to us that we take for granted. Tear glands, for example, keep our eyes moist and clear. What most of us think of as "real glands" are the endocrines. These stimulate growth and reproduction and their function colours the way we look and the way we feel. They act like tiny squirt bottles, shooting powerful secretions into the blood. Among the miracle workers are the pituitary, in your head, just above your eyebrows; the thyroid and the parathyroid in your throat; the thymus a little lower in your chest; the adrenals and the pancreas under your rib cage. All these wonderful gizmos – including your ovaries – work to keep you alive and kicking. The thyroid is mainly in charge of metabolism, the pituitary controls growth of bones and activity of sex glands. The pancreas supplies insulin plus secretions which aid digestion. The adrenals manufacture adrenaline and cortisone. You already know what the ovaries do (and thank Heaven for them) they manufacture oestrogen which makes you feminine, happy and content. But did you know you also manufacture male hormones to keep you in balance? And – though it seems peculiar – these male hormones help keep you sexy too (fair's fair though, men also have some female hormones but obviously the balance is different).

Of all the glands perhaps the pituitary is boss. Over the years a woman and her pituitary play a sort of ping pong. As a girl enters her teen years or even earlier, every 28 days this miracle-worker sends out a command "Go girl!" and releases an egg into her uterus. If the egg doesn't meet up with some cute wriggling sperm, it shrugs its shoulders and drifts out. And the cycle begins again.

Stand in awe of this amazing machine! When a girl reaches womanhood, the automatic switch clicks on to allow her to reproduce other human bodies. (Wouldn't it be wonderful if your blender could replace itself?)

And later in life, when child-bearing years end, another command goes out from headquarters – "Mission accomplished!" There may be a few re-adjustments at this time but the body soon regains its balance.

Other glands pitch in to take over most of the work of the retired ovaries and for a sensible, healthy woman, life goes on better than ever. With no small children around, new careers often beckon. With the shadow of unwanted pregnancy laid to rest, a woman may well develop a new twinkle in her eye.

So to top it all off, working as hard as a man, ensuring the continuation of the human race, juggling responsibilities like a circus acrobat, a woman STILL has the strength and vigour to outlast a man by at least five years.

Aren't women wonderful?

It's a bit scary being the owner of the World's Most Miraculous Machine. But YOU are securely in the driver's seat. You're going to take good care of this miracle of Celestial Engineering by providing it with the best fuel, with good maintenance routine and regular checkups. You learn to operate it at a reasonable speed, keeping the engine oiled and the moving parts moving.

Just remember, gals, despite such miracles as heart transplants and plastic surgery, this is one machine you can't really turn in for a new model. It is one to a customer – and it's built to last you a lifetime.

Dealing With "Age"

When it comes to dealing with age, our main problem, oddly enough, stems from "other people". Family, friends, magazines, television and all other influences remind us that we are "middle-aged," then "golden – aged" and "a senior citizen" and should act accordingly. The misconception is that a woman must undergo mental and physical torture at menopause, that at sixty, aches, pains and bifocals must not only be a way of life but the main topic of conversation. There is even the astonishing myth that women of advanced years can only enjoy love and sex vicariously through romance novels and soap operas.

Of course the "Grandma" image is convenient for children and grandchildren. Grandma is expected to be there whenever sons and daughters want to escape from parental responsibilities and obviously it suits the offspring to keep the status quo as status as possible.

Amazingly, if Grandma does revolt she finds her family still loves her and is secretly proud that the "old girl" has opted to lead her own life. With your family grown up and independent, surely this is the time to pour your energies into beginning a new life phase with a more glamorous, sexy image, to do what you've always wanted to do, go where you want to go, take up new hobbies, explore a new career, be ready to enjoy the full flowering of womanhood.

Without love we are incomplete, we need love – the love of our children, the love of our friends and the love of a good man. But nothing comes without effort. We must be prepared for mental housecleaning; we must study all the ways science and art can help us look our best, feel our best, function our best.

Today is the first day of the rest of your life. Are you ready for the challenge? Let's begin by sweeping a few dusty cobwebs from the corners of our minds — particularly those that prevent the total enjoyment of one of woman's greatest gifts – full sexual love.

Case History: Viola

Let us introduce our friend Viola, sane, secure, sexy and sixty. You meet so many Violas these days, good women all, solid citizens, their hand-bags heavy with photographs of the world's most beautiful grandchildren. So what makes women like Viola different?

THEY DON'T BUY THE MYTH THAT THEIR BEST DAYS WERE IN THE DIM, DISTANT PAST, AND THAT THEY ARE IN REALITY WAITING IN THE WINGS UNTIL THE GREAT DIRECTOR IN THE SKY CALLS ON THEM FOR THEIR FINAL APPEARANCE...

They don't feel responsible for everything that goes wrong, nor the compulsion to make everything go right. They keep healthy and trim, dress wisely, and use makeup artfully.

When someone – usually one of their own children – hints that it is unbecoming to go back to college to study Archaeology, demonstrate to save the manatees, take a trip through the Grenadines or dine with a charming young man, the Violas of this world respond with an innocent-eyed "WHY?".

"Because it doesn't look right at your age", is a pretty weak argument. One seventy-ish girl we know, on announcing that she was taking scuba lessons answered a brutal "Granny you should act your age", with "I am — so live with it, my darlings".

But our Viola wasn't always so liberated. She had been married for twenty-seven years to a nice, stodgy, kind man, who had been brought up by stern religious parents, who (like her own) had been taught that sex was intended by God for procreation and decent people used it for nothing else.

Naturally, it wasn't supposed to be fun. (Actually, Andy found it fun but tried not to let Viola know – his pure decent Viola who he was defiling for the sake of progeny.)

Viola, a virgin at marriage, went along with this. Andy was such a nice guy. He bought her roses, told her she was beautiful, never looked at another woman and she thought she was the luckiest woman alive, with all the romance she had read about in romantic novels. The furtive little sexual bouts were something a good wife took in her stride; she regarded them, perhaps, in the same light as she regarded the baby's dirty diapers or a sink full of dishes, something unpleasant to deal with as quickly as possible.

But even then, Viola had doubts. Her friend Amy hinted of the excitement of going to bed with a man and how much she got out of it. Another friend, Esme, admitted that she too enjoyed "the marital act". She said she couldn't help "crying out when it hits me". Esme, Viola believed, was a good woman. Was there something more to be enjoyed with her perfect husband? If other husbands did these things with wives they obviously respected, and the wives thought it was great fun, why wasn't it happening to her?

Viola looked at her nude body in a full-length mirror. Of course! Now she knew what was wrong – her hips were too big, her neck was too short, and she was, in fact, ugly. She completely forgot that Elizabeth Taylor's handsome Richard Burton had described her as "a small dumpy woman". All Viola saw was that she was inadequate. She was ashamed at being less than perfect. She didn't stop to think that nobody she knew was perfect – nobody at all, including Amy and Esme.

Still, nothing ventured, nothing gained! Viola set out to change her appearance. Exercises narrowed her hips and tightened her arms, posture practice gave her a pretty neckline – but Viola was sure she was still imperfect. She was not, in short, in love with herself; and not being in love with herself, she could not "allow" anyone else to love her physically. She even rationalized Andy's bursts of sexual activity by thinking "it is his duty as a husband – no doubt he is thinking about someone else all the time."

Poor Viola, happy housewife on the outside, desperately unhappy on the inside. Then Andy died of a heart attack at the age of 48. Obviously Viola's sex life was over.

Months later, Esme invited Viola out on a double date. Viola was immediately attracted to John, a tall, jovial guy with touches of grey in his hair and a fine sense of humour. After a delightful evening, John kissed her goodnight and something strange happened, Viola felt a bit dizzy, and a whole lot excited. Soon, to her shame, she was "going all the way" and the miracle was John didn't find her body repulsive and he hadn't lost all respect for her; in fact he was soon talking about marriage.

Viola looked in her full-length mirror again – she was still no Venus de Milo, but the sparkle in her eye had been put there by John. Viola did something else. In dark glasses and an old hat pulled down over her ears she daringly went to "one of those shops" where sex manuals were on sale, and did some late-night reading...

We met Viola for lunch recently, and found her smiling. "It's so strange," she said. "I love John, he's a wonderful man but I also love going to bed with him every night if possible. I never knew sex could be so much fun." Her expression sobered, "Tell me honestly, do you disapprove?"

Disapprove? We're out there cheering for Viola and her new man and for all the other sweet, sexy sixties who have learned how to combine romantic love and sexual love for the greatest relationship ever!

But it isn't easy. Why do we say that? Well, dears, come with us along memory lane and we'll show you what we mean.

Learning To Let Go

There are two words between which women over sixty must learn to differentiate; they are "duty" and "guilt". The reason – women in this age group have shouldered more guilt than any other generation in history. Our grandmothers knew all about duty.

Who decided what "duty" was?

God.

There was no room for debate.

For our grandmothers, duty meant to cook, sew, raise children, keep them clean and clothed, send them to school and church and submit to the lustful desires of their husbands.

Bad luck in our grandmother's time was blamed on the Devil, not on Grandma. But those of us born in the first half of the twentieth century had discovered psychology – Heaven help us! In our more "enlightened" time, there was no place to hide. Mummy was to blame for everything.

Did hubby drink and take up with other women? Something was obviously lacking in 'wifey'. (When the same thing happened to Grandma, she was considered a tragic, wronged figure.) Did a child turn bad? Obviously Mummy has bruised his tender psyche. (In Grandma's time such a disaster was the work of the Devil.) So since we were now guilty of almost everything, it followed that we had to be punished.

Sometimes we punished ourselves by denying ourselves simple pleasures like taking a day off with our feet up. Sometimes we punished ourselves subconsciously by denying ourselves sexual pleasures. Surely a Mummy who had produced less than perfect children, or failed to keep her husband away from painted ladies was ready for Hell! How could we have an orgasm when Junior was a "druggie" and daughter had lost three jobs in a row?

So lying there in the double bed, our minds were certainly not on our bodies. By the time all of our sins of omission and commission had raced through our minds, hubby was yawning and saying "was it alright for you dear?"

Obviously, if we are going to enjoy a new love affair, this guilt must be banished completely. We'll continue to be good Grannies but we'll refuse to be held responsible for EVERYTHING! We'll, instead, concentrate on being responsible for ourselves.

Another reason some of us can't relax completely when we make love is because we are not in love with ourselves. We are secretly ashamed of how we look and we feel inadequate. "How could this man in my bed possibly find me attractive?" we ask ourselves, forgetting, presumably that the fact that he IS THERE should tell you something.

Be honest now, who do you know that looks absolutely perfect? (Well yes, Sophia Loren and Lauren Bacall looked pretty fabulous at your age.) Forget the goal of absolute perfection. As one astute gentleman pointed out, "It ain't what you got, it's what you do with what you got that counts!"

OF COURSE you're going to make yourself look your best, but while you're making the effort, don't down-grade the material you're starting out with.

Having gotten this far in life, you must be doing something right!

In the Sunday Gleaner, (June, 1989) actor Tom Selleck says:

"Women, I think, get better as they get older. To me, what's attractive in a woman is reflected in the way she feels about herself. She may not be the most physically beautiful woman in the world, but she becomes attractive by the way she carries herself and thinks about herself – or doesn't think about herself."

Remember When? . . .

Cynthia writes about growing up in the twenties and thirties

One of the greatest obstacles to a happy sex life for many women now in their seventies and eighties is that they were brought up to believe that romance and sex were entirely different things, and never the twain could meet.

My generation was romantic. Romance was the best part of marriage, seen as a natural progression from the proposal, the wedding gown, and the magic moment of saying "I do" (without really understanding what the "do" included). You tossed the wedding bouquet to your very best friend. The other part of marriage was something you participated in as a good sport so your husband could enjoy his male rights and you could have darling little babies to cuddle and dress up.

Now, of course, we know that love is a more complicated business and that when sex and romance go together like bread and jam, the result is marvellous.

Actually, love in its broadest sense may not be concerned with sex at all. Parsons may truly love their flocks, and statesmen might truly love their countries.

I am certain that good nurses love their patients and dedicated teachers love their little students, runny noses and all. I know and I'm sure you know that people who love each other platonically, quite often, are people who work together and are deeply committed to their professions.

The subject of this chapter, however, is love between adult male and female human beings, mixing romance and sex. This is sometimes a difficult achievement for women of my generation and I will tell you why.

The problem was that our mothers believed that we should be protected from any knowledge of sex until ready for marriage or, at the very least, by the age of eighteen, when all decent girls were married anyway. At the same time they always seemed to expect the worst of us. After an evening in mixed teenage company the conversation would go something like this:

Mother: "Did you do anything nasty?"

Daughter: "Like what Mummy?"

Mother: "Never you mind!"

The height of pornography in my extreme youth was a little book called "Marjorie May's Twelfth Birthday," distributed free by the Kotex Company, makers of an early brand of sanitary pads. All you had to do was send in a coupon and the book would be sent to you in a plain wrapper that wouldn't fool your mother for a minute. (One little kid named Maureen had managed to get the first copy in our gang, and would lend it to you for one day if you promised to be her best friend for life.) The subject matter, as you have guessed, was menstruation or, as the big girls called it, "The Curse".

Not only did the booklet reveal the tingling truth about what happened on Marjorie May's twelfth birthday, it even had a little sketch of Marjorie May's insides and you couldn't get much dirtier than that!

Any reasonable person might suppose that our mothers would have welcomed this innocuous little tract which said nothing to suggest that "being sick" or "having your monthlies" had anything to do with S-E-X. But only a few mothers were that enlightened, mothers who played bridge and wore Tangee lipstick.

Even before reading Marjorie May, I realized something mysterious was going on in my own home. Once a month my mother locked me out of the laundry room (where I was usually slave labour) to manage our old brass washing machine strictly by herself.

And after dark, I could see them from my bedroom window, those pale white flannelette flags which spelt – WOMAN! We little girls compared notes, put two and two together, and by the time our mothers were forced to tell us the truth, we already knew. But we listened with innocent eyes and sealed lips for we had learned the first rule about coping with your mother about sex – LIE!

"Your troubles have started now!" was the usual gloomy introduction to womanhood. Fortunately my nutty Aunt Lill was on hand when I first displayed my spotted nightgown. She slapped me on the back, chortled, and said, "Congratulations, you're a woman now – give us a kiss, love."

From then on it wasn't all plain sailing however. We discussed in whispers the ominous stories about some unfortunate woman who had "ruined her life". We were confused by the fact that pregnant ladies tried to hide their "condition" in billowing smocks. When this strategy could no longer conceal the awful truth that they had done something very dirty, they stayed in their homes, emerging only when extreme circumstances made it necessary to creep outside to join other (pure as snow) people. And yet, when a sweet little baby emerged, there was rejoicing; gifts, flowers, hugs and kisses were showered on the new, completely pure Mummy. So we wondered: did grown-ups really believe babies came from storks or cabbage patches?

Marguerite writes about growing up in the forties and fifties.

Although I grew up a generation later than Cynthia, my experiences as a child and my introduction to the world of growing up and sex were almost as shrouded in mystery, legend and superstition. S-E-X was not even spelled out in our house, it was not even mentioned. I grew up in a comfortable, happy home presided over by wonderful adoring parents determined to shield my sisters and I from the harsh realities of the cruel world.

Jamaica had no television until 1962 and our parents made sure that the movies we were permitted to attend were carefully monitored. So we were exposed to Walt Disney and such magnificent musicals as "The Student Prince" and "Singing in the Rain".

We were surrounded by pets and we learned to ride horses and bicycles and do all the things nice children did.

My mother, a registered nurse who had travelled extensively, gave up her career when she married and dedicated her life exclusively to taking care of her husband and family and, she was, without a doubt, the best mother in the world. Our British Victorian grandparents (who stayed married for 53 years) were eager to impart advice on the evil intents of men and of improper dress and makeup – which my grandmother continually pointed out were "cheap and degrading and only worn by loose women with no background". I remember scrambling to remove lipstick when her car appeared at the gate, and among my most vivid recollection was the time she caught my sister and me playing Ludo with two teenage boys we had met at a party.

I was then sixteen. It was broad daylight. Both our parents were at home and our ever-present Nanny was in attendance when Grandma barged in. Everyone was roundly told off and the young "men" were ushered out "since the children must be protected from the evils of mankind".

But childhood and puberty were times of a hundred contradictions. That same Grandma practised witchcraft as a hobby and was a great believer in the occult and black magic that held us children in great awe and held her in high esteem at the Knutsford Park Racetrack for picking winners! The lines between good and evil were sometimes difficult to follow.

In our teens, our encounters with the opposite sex were confined to well-chaperoned parties. At home, sex, war and other "unpleasant" things were never discussed in front of "the children". And, at our very proper girls' school, our Biology classes skirted around the subject of sex and the reproductive organs.

My father, a world traveller and brilliant international marine surveyor, had been brought up in a rural Presbyterian household in Scotland. The very mention of feminine underwear embarrassed him – and he was not alone in this regard. No proper father of our generation discussed anything "to do with the feminine body". And certainly, any discussion between male and female was taboo in mixed company. My father constantly pointed out to us the unfortunate "plight" of his aging cousins who had remained spinsters and, either consciously or unconsciously, pounded into our receptive teenage minds that marriage was the only "proper" life for a lady.

"Before you marry you are my responsibility," he would say. "After you marry you will be your husband's responsibility." Nobody suggested that, as an adult, I might want to be responsible for myself.

Although the charts in Biology class imparted some sparse information and the movies showed girls and boys kissing, I was eighteen before I actually realized what Sleeping Beauty and Prince Charming were up to when they went off together to pursue marital bliss. In the meantime, sex was strictly a "no-no" and, although it was whispered about in ladies washrooms, it was considered to be one of those things that you "didn't do until you were properly married".

My later teenage life included double-dates with a sister or friend. There was some petting or necking that evoked strange feelings that were quickly suppressed "in case things got out of hand". Then came my big awakening.

I had left to study art and dancing in the big, wicked city of Montreal and went to work at the Arthur Murray Ballroom studio where dancers far older and more experienced than I smoked and drank and pursued sexual excitement with no inhibitions whatsoever. It may have been a rude awakening but it was an enlightening one. My three years in that city exposed me to the real world — of crime and violence and a complete education as to how "the other half" lived. I discovered that S-E-X was not all that mysterious, in fact, some people even enjoyed it and discussed it openly – and they weren't even married. I returned to my little protected world in Jamaica, from time to time, and found my parents had grown much more liberal. My mother in particular was more open in her discussions but my father was still perturbed that I still was a "spinster" and that at twenty-one years of age I had gone to live alone in Bermuda.

I was busily shaking off my inhibitions. But early training persists: I knew I should not be branded "a loose woman" in small island society. I opened my own dance studio in a Jamaican hotel, became engaged several times, started writing, sold out my studio and took off on an extended tour of Europe and West Africa (where I almost got married).

When I finally came home to Jamaica I took up modelling and TV work, continued writing, dancing and art on a commercial scale and began dating on a mature level. I still found I was subconsciously searching for Mr. Right, that perfect man with whom I would spend my life in perpetual and proper bliss. The only answer was marriage – marriage took the sin out of S-E-X.

It was only much later that I discovered that Prince Charmings get older, Sleeping Beauties get sexier, and sex becomes better and better with every passing year.

Dispelling The Myths of Childhood

It must be done but it certainly isn't easy. The woman who is able to learn that sex and romantic love are part of one glorious gift of life is a happy woman. A mature woman can initiate sex, show her man she is ready and waiting, and that he alone is the object of her very feminine desires.

Men are extremely grateful when such a woman enters their lives. We discover that men are not lusting beasts desiring only to sully a good woman's life but ordinary humans, just like us – maybe brought up with some of the same myths we were, and perhaps even a bit nervous – as we are – about the ability to perform. So let us live like the mature women we know. If they can do it, so can we!

Case History: Hannah

Born into a strict Jewish family in Aruba, Hannah had dutifully become a Jewish princess. Mama began looking for a suitable prince while Hannah still had braces on her teeth – but Hannah went WRONG. At 18, she got pregnant by and married a poor but romantic genius; Jewish (to his credit) but radical (to Mama's undying shame). Fortunately, he died of tuberculosis and too much poetry when their daughter Rebecca was only four. Hannah's next choice was even worse. She eloped with a Swede!

Mama called in the Rabbi for solace, and since his was a reformed congregation, he told her to look on the bright side. Olaf had a job and he could always become a Jew (privately the Rabbi sighed; first a 'no good nick' and next a goy!) He was not surprised when it turned out that Olaf, absentmindedly, had left a wife in Sweden and departed after the wedding ceremony, taking the better pieces of silver from among the gifts.

Hannah's third husband ("at last!") was the answer to Mama's prayers; a good Jewish lawyer serving corporations who paid him handsomely out of what he saved them in taxes. Hannah was determined that THIS MARRIAGE WOULD WORK!

And so it did until she surprised her lawyer husband in his office. Her first impulse was laughter at the rhythmic flopping of Myron's testicles against the rounded bottom of his junior partner. Her second impulse (training tells) was to call her own lawyer.

One hundred thousand dollars later, she arrived in Trinidad, bought two condos – one to live in and one for income. Hannah was now fifty-four, her body and soul had suffered over the years and she had yet to experience the culmination the sex manuals promised.

She began to ache all over. Her knees began to swell. "You've got arthritis" her doctor said firmly. "You're getting old. So am I and I live with it. Take these pills and live with it."

But Hannah had always been a thinker. She read everything she could find about arthritis and found a dozen confusing theories – but almost all the experts considered that stress was a contributing factor. Physical stress could be caused by major surgery, disease, bad nutrition – the list seemed endless. Emotional stress was caused by everything from the loss of a loved one to a change in environment. Some stress was good, the stress of exercising, lovemaking, or completing a project. When Hannah read the list of bad stressors, it seemed she was reading the story of her life. She knew she must conquer stress if she wanted hope to improve her condition.

She took her vitamins, put herself on a healthful diet, and took long walks on the beach. After her two-hour walk she noticed she came home and slept like a baby. She stuck to her diet of vegetables, fruit and fish and, to keep her mind off the chocolate chip cookies she was missing, she joined a sketching class. She got a lot of help from a handsome young Chinese Trinidadian whose easel was set up next to hers. Hannah hardly noticed when the pains of arthritis began to go away. She felt happier and healthier than ever before.

Now Hannah and Louis have added a studio to the condo they share. Hannah paints watercolours she sells to an appreciative clientele, while Louis puts his Chinese ancestry to use in the kitchen, turning out delicious feasts of steamed vegetables and delicately flavoured chicken and fish. Because his practice as an architect is profitable, there is money for romantic trips to Paris or Rome. Hannah sticks to her health routine, has given up smoking and drinks only a little wine. One day each week she goes to bed at sundown with a nice trashy novel. She emerges at sunup dewy-fresh and if Louis hasn't left for his office she can usually be persuaded to go back to bed for a little while.

Hannah is a happy, healthy woman. With Louis she has seen the flowing of sexual enjoyment and romantic love. Now approaching seventy, she looks twenty years younger and Louis has never been happier. Hannah refused to play the role custom had written for her – and produced her own hit production.

Hannah has become a star.

Doing The Most With What You've Got

BEFORE REJUVENATION BEGINS

When Hannah, our happy lady of the previous pages, set out to restructure her life, she conducted a little experiment in the privacy of her own room – something we should all do from time to time, just to remind us just how important it is to keep our bodies in tiptop shape, to note our good points and learn how to emphasize them, and to recognize our deficiencies and learn how to minimize them. Notice what all your prettiest features are – every woman is different. Many curvaceous women have beautiful slim calves and ankles. Generally shoulders are great survivors and so are wrists. Backs and bottoms often outlast tummies and tits but you can practise sitting, standing, bending or twisting to minimize the figure faults you discover. Let us remember the great Sarah Bernhardt who mesmerized men with her charms despite a wooden leg and the French courtesan who, when asked at what age a woman should stop enjoying sex, answered, "Why ask me? I'm only sixty-five".

Remember, however, disguising faults is one thing, eliminating them is another. As the members of Alcoholics

"It is gravity that pulls down the corners of your lips..."

"Plan to defeat gravity..."

Anonymous pray: "God, give me the strength to change the things I can change, to accept the things I can't change, and the wisdom to know the difference".

Having accepted what we can't change and determined to change what we can change, let us think of ourselves as wonderfully unique people to whom the years on the calendar have no meaning.

DEFY GRAVITY – AND YOU'RE ON YOUR WAY TO DEFYING AGE

So many scientific books have been written about the process of aging that we will not attempt to go into the medical details as to why and how it happens to every living thing on planet earth, and why it occurs more slowly in some creatures than others.

To sum it up in simple terms, advancing age involves changes in hormone balance and the break-down of cells in the body. These alterations in body chemistry bring about the gradual physical changes that we have come to associate with progressive aging.

Today, this process is considered no more nor less than a degenerative disease which, although it cannot be prevented, can be slowed down and its debilitating effects significantly reduced. Many of its more unflattering symptoms can be greatly alleviated through such simple and natural methods as the development of correct breathing, exercise, diet and elimination patterns; and the discarding of unhealthy habits such as smoking and the excessive consumption of drugs and alcohol.

THE FIRST STEPS TOWARDS DEFYING GRAVITY

There is no doubt that gravity plays a big role in setting the pace at which the signs of aging emerge. Does this mean that if we were to leave this planet in a space capsule and float in a gravity-free environment, we would remain forever young and return to earth like modern-day Rip Van Winkles to resume life at the same age we were when we left? When a spacecraft is orbiting the earth, the sun can rise and set every fifteen minutes, days pass very quickly at that rate and yet those aboard the shuttle don't change in appearance. Time and space, in other words, are only relevant if measured by our earthly parameters.

Well, if we remain here on Earth, (and who really wants to be entombed in an ageless vacuum in outer space for a few decades when the action is here and now) we can still address the problem of gravity and do what we can to overcome it; hence our own little plan of action to which we refer (for better or worse) as our Anti-gravity Crusade.

WHAT IS GRAVITY?

When we talk about gravity in this particular context, we are referring not only to that force that has been continually pulling our bodies downwards for decades, we are also talking about gravity of an equally debilitating kind – gravity of the mind, of the spirit and the soul.

It is gravity of one kind or another that drags us down into a chair and encourages us to remain sedentary. It is gravity that pulls down the corners of our mouths; it is gravity that encourages our backs to bend and our shoulders to slump and our bodies to sag – need we go on?

THE BATTLE WITH GRAVITY BEGINS!
PLAN TO WIN!

Smile! Watch the corners of your mouth go upwards and outwards; the more you smile and laugh, the less your face sags, the more your facial muscles work in a positive way, the better they support your face and the less your age is noticed by those around you.

There's a lot to smile about. Think of amusing anecdotes and situations – a good comedy movie can keep us smiling for days, watch the happy antics of a cute puppy or kitten, there is humour in almost everything if you take the trouble to appreciate the interesting things around you. If your surroundings seem drab and colourless, use your imagination to add a few bright touches that can inspire happy moods. The mind itself is a wonderful source of fun and happiness. Put on some music, drift into reveries of beautiful thoughts and watch your face in the mirror as you think. True beauty comes from within. You can never be an attractive person if your thoughts are filled with hate and your face is twisted in a perpetual scowl. Some people drive you crazy? Don't let a frown spoil your face – laugh at them. If you allow the people around you to upset you and see the bad side of every situation, your gravity of mind will reflect on your face in ugly expressions. Were you grinding your teeth at that pushy lady in the supermarket checkout counter? Stop and picture her slipping on a wet floor and tipping ass-over-tea-kettle to display her bloomers! And Smile!

Intolerance and impatience can become debilitating habits that can rob your face of all its naturally pleasant vitality and make you a prime target for the forces of gravity.

Learn to see the good side of everyone and the funny side of life. Love and humour can be contagious. Share your laughter, not your anger. Try to be the "carrier" of good humour and victory over gravity can be yours.

As the saying goes, "always be happy when you can for no one loves a sorrowful man" – or woman.

ACTION!!!

Now we have begun to develop our anti-gravity action programme for the mind, let's see what we can do to conquer and overcome the effects of gravity on the body.

First of all, get up and s-t-r-e-t-c-h! Stand as tall as you can and feel the ribcage lift as you stretch one out-stretched hand above the other, as you reach for the ceiling. Lift the chin. Feel as though you have a string attached to the top of your head pulling you steadily upward.

Doesn't that feel g-o-o-d? Now stretch both arms above your head and clasp your hands with the palms stretched upwards. Keep pressing as though you were trying to place them flat on the ceiling. Relax and repeat.

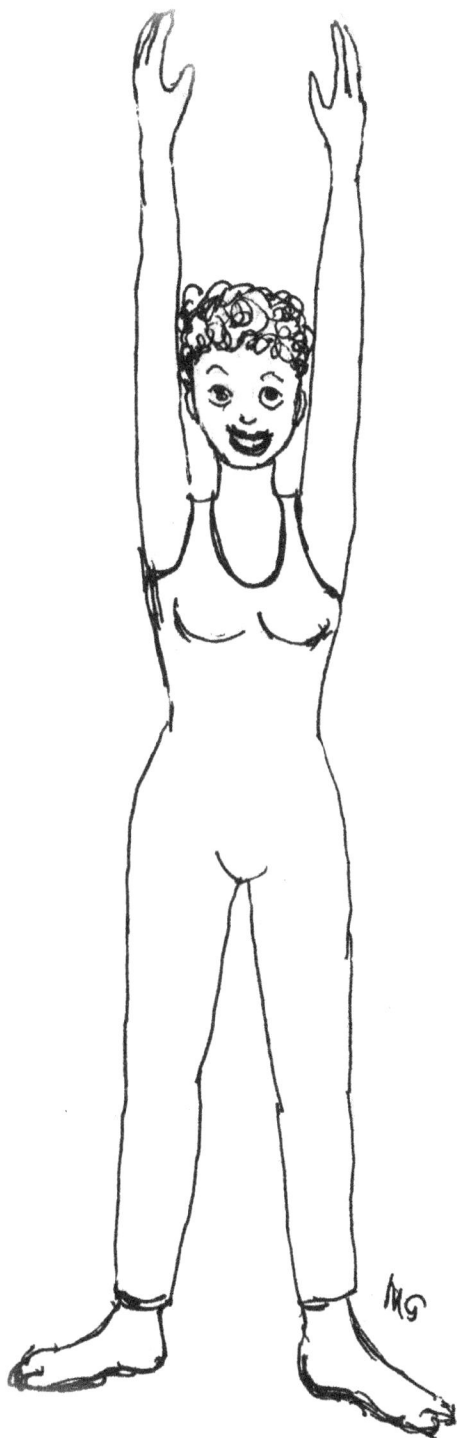

"Get up and stretch"

If you do these simple exercises regularly (and as often as possible) you will be several steps ahead of the game in the process of cheating gravity of its control over your life and your looks.

TURN THE WORLD UPSIDE DOWN!

Ancient Chinese medicine often included the practice of inversion as a remedy of variety of physical and mental complaints. Some present day medical procedures in China still call for anti-gravity measures.

If you go swimming, you are practising the art of weightlessness because as long as your body remains in the water, you are being fully supported.

The ancient Chinese and the health-oriented Indian yogi went a step further and advocated taking the weight off the body entirely by placing the body in an inverted (upside down) position. This form of complete reversion of the pull of gravity on the body system and its precious organs has been used as a cure for everything from chronic lung congestion to heart and circulatory complaints.

Over the past few years, we have come to appreciate the benefits that can be derived from making use of this particular body position. Not only does it completely relax the lower body and its circulatory system, it sends extra blood and oxygen to the head and upper body, stimulating the skin, brightening the complexion and revitalizing the brain cells.

HOW TO DO IT

If you have a serious back problem, have never exercised before, or if the idea of hoisting your legs up into the air sounds completely crazy, you can achieve some of the benefits by using an adjustable slant board available in sporting goods stores. Tip it at a comfortable angle and use it for relaxation for fifteen to twenty minute periods with your feet as high above your head as possible. If such a board is not available, you can still score a few points against gravity by placing pillows under your bottom and putting your legs straight up and feet against the wall.

For those adventurous ladies who really want to get serious about fitness and are game to lift those hips skyward, here is how to do the shoulder stand, recommended by those ancient Chinese doctors.

1) Lie flat on a large towel or mat.
2) Extend arms straight down at your sides.
3) Bend both knees and lift them towards your chest.
4) Place your hands under your hips and, resting on your elbows, lift your hips upward as you straighten your legs.
5) To come down, bend your knees and lower the small of your back to the floor first and then hips. Straighten your legs and your back position. Return to position 2.

Note: *If during this exercise you feel that you are about to topple over, just bend your knees until you regain your balance.*

WORD OF CAUTION

Please never do this or any other exercise directly after eating or drinking. All exercises, and particularly those done in an inverted position, must be done on an empty stomach. Need we tell you why?

Don't you wish you had known all this when you were thirty-five? It is never too early – and never too late – to begin the fight against that inevitable age-maker, gravity.

Case History: Angie

A group of prominent scientists decided, back in 1988, to do a computer study to discover "the most beautiful body in showbiz". After assessing pictures of faces, figures and vital statistics of stars like Bo Derek, Dolly Parton, Linda Evans and Victoria Principal, this particular study gave top marks to the star of the TV Series "Policewoman" – Angie Dickenson – who was fifty-five years young.

How does she feel about men? "The men I like", she said in a press interview, "no matter what their age, all have some things in common. They are always good-looking, amusing, witty, intelligent, cool and interesting. The nice thing about reaching my age is that I no longer have to go out looking for guys like that. They seem to have the sense to come and find me".

Do Those Tell-tale Signs of Aging Really Have to be?

Have you ever stopped to think how people judge a woman's age? Just what specific aspects of hair, face and body suggest that a woman is thirty-ish, forty-ish or older?

Think, for a moment, of the people you know. What is it about their appearance that suggests their age?

In many instances, the age of a particular person may never have been important to you at all unless you were trying to describe them to somebody else. As far as your personal relationships go, you like and associate with someone because of an engaging personality, someone combining humour with wisdom – someone who makes YOU feel good. The age of the person is never a deciding factor in any relationship of real value.

Since self-improvement is what this chapter is all about and since all women feel more confident if they look better, let us examine some of the more unflattering physical problems we are likely to encounter, and suggest some solutions.

EXCESSIVE WEIGHT CAN MAKE A WOMAN LOOK OLDER AT ANY AGE

If you have not been careful about eating and drinking and lead a sedentary existence, the chances are you

"A woman can look old at any age"

are not too happy about your present physical condition; and as the years pass, you are finding it harder and harder to pull yourself together. The time for change is NOW, a change in diet and lifestyle.

Turn on the radio and start to dance! Get up and move around! S-T-R-E-T-C-H! WALK!

If you have been forced into a sedentary way of life by some medical condition, you can still move your head and arms to music. Besides making you feel better, exercise of any kind helps you replace the calcium your body requires to build the muscle and bone tissue you need to increase your rate of metabolism and shed excess pounds. Sedentary people lose calcium quickly, bones weaken and break and teeth decay. Don't let this happen to YOU!

There has been so much written about the dread condition known as osteoporosis and the importance of taking calcium supplements to prevent it, that we won't go into it here. But we repeat, without exercise your bones will continue to lose calcium. Inactivity can cause rapid bone and muscle degeneration, so you must decide to get up and out if you are to give your spine the strength it needs to keep you upright.

ENLARGED VEINS AND CELLULITE

These two main problems faced by older women are really not age-related but, rather, body-condition related. If poor circulation is your problem and your enlarged veins fall into the varicose category, you probably inherited the tendency to develop weak valves and surgery may be necessary and desirable. Very fine capillaries that surface and become prominent can be treated with injections and the procedure is relatively simple. Whatever the complexity of the problem, you can certainly help to improve it by avoiding long hours of standing, wearing the correct support-hosiery and raising your feet above your head whenever possible.

Do remember that heat of any kind, including hot baths and steam treatments will dilate the blood vessels and make them appear more pronounced.

Cellulite is a breakdown of elastin, fibroblast and collagen network in the skin and this condition is worsened by lack of exercise. The best remedy we can recommend is a body-firming programme of healthy diet and exercise, and a twice-daily regimen of stimulation. Splashes of skin freshener or the application of a body-toning gel followed by a gentle circular massage of collagen or elastin skin cream can be helpful. If you want to see really positive results, you will need to couple this daily treatment with a serious exercise programme to firm the muscles and tissue in the affected areas.

If you are overweight, don't believe the "miraculous" claims of weight-loss products that promise a magic pill will melt the pounds away. Read the small print: "For best results must be combined with regular exercise and sensible diet". The only way to lose that extra flab is to pursue a well-balanced, low salt, low sugar, low starch, high fibre diet, along with exercise. Half-way measures simply won't work.

You will only conquer cellulite if you have a determined will to do so. You must set about reconditioning your mind and body, with a will to succeed.

GREY HAIR IS SEEN AS AN OBVIOUS GIVE-AWAY

There is hardly a human being – male or female – who does not panic over the first signs of grey. Some notice in their twenties, some much later in life, and there are others who retain their rich youthful natural colour until they die of old age. Grey hair can look distinguished on some people, but on others it gives the impression of middle-age.

Should grey hair be camouflaged or left natural? We feel that women look younger with tinted hair – colour adds life and vitality to any scene. Just as the leaves and flowers fade, our skin and our hair lose colour as we mature. We believe in defying Nature by adding the missing colour. Just as the movie technicians breathe new life into ancient black-and-white movies with modern colour techniques, we can bring back lost richness to hair and skin with modern hair tints and makeup.

If you are about to colour your hair for the first time, do seek the advice of a recommended professional hairdresser and try to bring your hair back to its natural shade or just one shade lighter. It is wise to stay with the softer ash tones and avoid harsh reds and very strong blacks. The new colour shampoos are easy to use, and if you are not happy with your first choice, it is relatively simple to make a change when the colour begins to fade.

If your hair is only showing silver streaks, you can create a dramatic effect by highlighting your natural streaks with a blonde rinse, turning your silver threads to gold.

Isn't modern science wonderful?

A more disturbing sign of aging is hair loss. This is more of a problem for men than women. Many women retain thick healthy hair all their lives, others suffer hair loss due to stress, poor nutrition, hormonal imbalance and other conditions. If you are losing your hair, get a medical opinion to find out what physical or mental problems can be causing it. It is common practice in our age group to put hair loss down to menopause, or old age, and regard it as inevitable, when we should be seeking ways to correct it. Proper hair care diet and good general health play a major role. We don't regard the: "Hair today – gone tomorrow" theory as unavoidable, unless the body suffers a major catastrophe.

Case History: Arlene

Arlene, at eighty-nine, was bemoaning hair loss after a hip operation, and she had finally resorted to wearing scarves to cover her head. This was not the wisest course of action since head ties and wigs inhibit normal circulation and potential hair regeneration. We could only make friendly suggestions but she followed them to the letter.

She began to massage her scalp every day by gently moving the skin back and forth with her finger-tips. She changed to a natural vitamin-based shampoo. She rested on her bed with her feet elevated on pillows to allow the blood to flow towards her scalp, and increased her intake of certain vitamins and minerals, with her doctor's permission.

We didn't see Arlene for several months. Then, one day, there was an excited phone call: Arlene was going to a hairdresser to have her hair trimmed. We are convinced that her success was mainly due to faith that the procedures WOULD work. But we suspect that the removal of the scarves that had interfered with blood circulation could have contributed to the re-growth of her hair. A positive attitude is a great asset as is the will to make a real effort towards self-improvement, regardless of age.

AGE SPOTS AND OTHER SKIN DISCOLORATIONS

Age spots and other skin discolorations simply represent a half century or less of sun and fun and other abuses of that valuable body covering. Sure, some skin blemishes are hereditary, as are some circulatory problems that show up later in life. But, as one doctor pointed out, if you look at the super-smooth, blemish-free areas of your body that have seldom, if ever, been exposed to sunlight, you can see what the rest of your body would have looked like if it had never suffered exposure to ultra-violet rays.

"Get yourself a glamorous hat!"

And the UV light from the sun, now intensified by Global Warming, is responsible for, not only so-called signs of aging but skin cancer for all age groups.

When we were young, nobody warned us that UV rays were linked to skin cancer or that later in life our skins would suffer from such exposure. So the damage has been done; so what can be done about it?

Well, first of all, get yourself a glamorous hat and a good sunscreen lotion (Nos. 30 or higher) to protect your precious skin. The myth that darker skins are naturally protected against UV rays is absolutely not true.

If tell-tale age spots are already appearing on hands, arms and face, you may want to consult a dermatologist. Please use sunscreens, long sleeves, cotton garden and driving gloves and other cover-ups unless you want those discolorations to get worse. Avoidance of direct sunlight must become a way of life.

WRINKLES ARE TRADITIONALLY CONSIDERED A SIGN OF AGE

Besides contributing to skin discoloration and skin cancer, UV rays can literally etch miles of deep lines into a normally smooth complexion. Just think how the sun can change a smooth grape into a wrinkled raisin. When we squint our eyes against the glare, we crease the surface of the face into massive crow's feet and other unflattering lines.

To make a head start in reducing the lines on your face, begin by investing in a good pair of sunglasses or ask your eye doctor to tint your prescription lenses for UV protection. Cheap sunglasses may leave you squinting just as badly as before.

How often do you have your eyes checked? A bi-annual check-up is really a good idea because glasses that no longer suit your requirements can cause further squinting, and later, wrinkles.

Do seek help in selecting attractive frames. Take a friend along to help you choose. Opt for the aluminium frames that feel light and cool and don't leave unflattering indentations on either side of your nose. If you have to wear glasses all the time, you could decide that contact lenses would suit you. These also come in very flattering tints that can brighten eye colour or give you the eye shade you've always dreamed of having. If your doctor suggests contacts, you might as well select the most glamorous you can find.

Please, never ever rub your eyes. Friction stretches the skin and causes unnecessary wrinkling and puffiness. It can also introduce bacteria that can cause serious problems later. If eyes itch, try to find out the cause. To relieve the itching, pat eyelids lightly with a cotton cosmetic pad saturated with eye lotion.

Don't discount the importance of exercise in maintaining good facial and body circulation. Every exercise that leaves you perspiring will act as a revitalizer and oxygenator for the skin – but please, if you care about your complexion, never exercise in bright sunlight or excessive heat.

"Choosing the glasses that are right for you"

While you are making all these positive efforts towards regenerating your skin, remember you can destroy the good you've done by continuing to smoke cigarettes. Apart from discolouring your teeth and skin and causing your face to squint and wrinkle, the smoke you ingest affects your mental alertness and your circulation. You can, in fact, de-activate up to fifteen percent of your normal blood supply to the skin and other parts of the body through carbon monoxide inhalation.

Quite aside from the health and beauty aspects, smoking can affect your popularity. Many health-conscious men are completely turned off by a smoking female. Moreover, now that more people are keeping their homes "smoke-free", the names of persistent smokers are often left off the guest list, particularly for dinner parties. Who needs this kind of social handicap?

POUCHES AROUND THE EYES

For some reason the under brow area tends to puff and droop and water-retention sometimes affects the area. If the puffiness is not too pronounced, you reduce it by applying cold compresses saturated with eye lotion. Another good home remedy is to cut a cucumber into wafer-thin slices, wrap it up and chill it in the refrigerator. Remove two pieces at a time and place one on each eye while you are relaxing.

A reduction of salt in the diet can alleviate water retention generally. If the puffiness persists, you may want to consider plastic surgery. Cosmetic surgery is expensive but we know several people who have regained self confidence after surgery. Unfortunately, the results are not permanent; in fact, the benefits can disappear very quickly if the skin is not cared for properly in the months after surgery.

NEGLECTED TEETH ARE A SIGN OF AGING

We all know the need for careful brushing and flossing after every meal and the importance of a twice-annual dental check-up to detect tooth and gum problems early. Never go to bed without brushing away the last remnant of a late night nibble or dose of medication. Your night time breath should be as sweet as the breath of spring to inspire your bed partner to greater heights of love-making. If your teeth are strong, make use of the natural tooth cleaners and plaque removers such as sticks of raw celery, carrots, unpeeled cucumbers and apples. Chewing on these exercises the jaw, helps to massage the gums and adds important vitamin supplements to your diet. Old-time Jamaicans cleaned their teeth with natural "chew stick", and it worked!

Getting Your Head Together

Dr. Hans Selye, who pioneered the study of stress and its effects on our bodies and minds, researched the mysterious ways in which stress works. He differentiated between positive and negative stress and gave us sensible rules to follow to avoid the negative onslaughts on mind and body.

All stress has an effect on us. Overwork causes stress. Loss of a loved one causes stress. Whenever the stock markets crash, no doubt the stress level rises worldwide; but, good things cause stress as well; winning a game of tennis, leading the Boston symphony, making love. Stress is not necessarily to be avoided. Exercise is stressful but beneficial. What Selye teaches is that we must make stress work FOR us and not against us.

Negative stress comes from overwork, illness, lack of rest, and worry. This type of stress, says the good doctor, becomes "dis-stress". Negative emotions – anger, grief, envy, and boredom – all cause dis-stress. Positive stress may result from working hard at something you like doing, exercising properly, or even enjoying a night out with friends. In fact, stress might be defined as doing what you enjoy while dis-stress is caused by doing something you don't enjoy. Most people who work hard doing work they love, seem to live longer. In short, some people are just too busy to find time to grow old.

But, you may say, how can you avoid that wrong kind of stress? Perhaps it's time to change your attitude. If you hate housework, can you develop another saleable talent so you can pay someone else to wash and do the dishes? Could you take a part time job as a receptionist or give piano lessons? Do you know apartment dwellers who need somebody to walk their dogs? Do they need a book keeper at the day-care centre? Meanwhile get the dis-stress work over with as quickly as possible and promise yourself a reward. When the blues hit you, walk away from them. Take a brisk stroll around the neighbourhood, take your books back to the library, call a friend and refuse to talk about anything that isn't cheerful.

Misery likes company but company doesn't like misery. There are some things nobody wants to hear about – your gallstone operation, the way your brother cheated you in your Dad's will, the fish vendor that overcharged you, why you will never speak to your cousin, Margo, ever again, or the bowel movements of your grandchildren.

Go out more, join a club, attend church, take up creative dance. When you have filled your life with interesting, useful and profitable things to do, you will be happier and healthier.

We repeat; stress is not just another name for nervous tension. Positive stress is part of living. Life is activity. Death is the end of activity. Receiving a letter with good news is stressful, the pulse quickens, we smile, and we breathe more quickly. A man who attracts us, looks in our direction, causes bells to ring and orchestras to play and our bodies react with a wonderful positive surge of energy. If we tried to remove all "stress" from our lives we would be well on the way to the undertaker.

Having accepted that there are two kinds of stress and having learned to welcome the positive kind, how do we cope with the dis-stress which results from a great disappointment, the trauma of a broken marriage, grief at the death of a loved one or fear of death itself?

There are certain religions that teach that everything that happens is pre-ordained and is the will of God, Allah, or Jah. No doubt people who believe this sincerely suffer less stress when disaster strikes but other religions and philosophies also offer ways of coping. The Seventh Day Adventists proclaim that the ills of the body are caused by mind and emotions. The Society of Friends (Quakers) seeks their Heaven deep inside themselves during meditation and suffers less from psychosomatic illnesses. We may not agree with some of their religious precepts but we can listen and learn to control our thinking and promote positive attitudes. "Always look on the bright side of life", an old song advises.

Yes, we all have our troubles, our aches and our pains but we are ALIVE.

"That's all very well," you may say, "but here I am with my bad back, my hearing aid and my ungrateful children; and my husband has run off with some floozy. I'm friendless and alone, and, on top of everything else, cucumbers give me heartburn".

Once again, remember that famous prayer, "Give me the strength to change what I can change, accept what I cannot change and the wisdom to know the difference". Once we accept what we are, we see ourselves realistically and lovingly and now we can work at what needs to be improved with a new enthusiasm. We are learning to appreciate ourselves, winning our own self-love and self-respect. Given this, the task of self-improvement becomes very much easier.

But wait a minute, it may be true that nothing makes big problems seem smaller than a good night's sleep – but even sleep can be a problem.

SLEEP YOUR TROUBLES AWAY

Some women find it hard to sleep even when their bodies are screaming for rest. At night we may toss and turn over all the mistakes we have made, the things we should have done and didn't and the things we did do and shouldn't have come back to haunt us as the moon rises.

Some women are simply bone tired trying to be three people at once – wife, mother, wage earner – since many women who work usually have such selfish reasons as paying for the groceries or sending their kids through school. But, in those wee small hours, there is no good angel to hold our hand and assure us that if everything that is wrong with our families is not

OUR fault, then obviously what is wrong with us is our mother's fault and so on back to Eve – so we might as well go to sleep and stop worrying. Even if we were to be blamed for everything there would be very little we could do about it at three o'clock in the morning.

We have the greatest trouble sleeping, oddly enough, when we are overtired. Fortunately, there are many aids to sleep. The most commonly used is the sleeping pill, which our generation was brought up to feel was sinful. The reasoning was:

- If you had a clear conscience you wouldn't need a pill to sleep.
- If you didn't have a clear conscience you didn't deserve to sleep.
- People who took sleeping pills were dope addicts anyway.

Let's take a more sensible approach. Sleeping pills, tranquilizers and anti-depressants are usually addictive to a greater or lesser degree. Many have unpleasant side effects as do other unnatural substances such as the polluted air we breathe and the over-processed foods we eat. Moreover, medication which puts you to sleep seldom gives the best level of rest. However, taken occasionally with a doctor's prescription, they can give a woman much needed rest when she has been under severe emotional pressure or physical strain; and sometimes the need for a good night's sleep outweighs the negativity of the side effects.

At the same time, there are other ways to lure the goddess of sleep. Among them: meditation, autohypnosis (you can learn how to do this through available books or recordings) and sometimes a bedtime glass of warm milk helps. And if we're still lying there worrying, remember this old proverb, "Don't cry over spilled milk".

If you are a wife and mother, you know that as long as you live you will have responsibilities towards your family. But giving to your loved ones must never be a twenty-four-seven task. There must still be hours reserved for you – to rest, to relax, to work at something you enjoy, to make love. The very enemies which may prevent sound sleep are the same ones that make it impossible to fall in love fully and completely.

Doing The Most With The Body You've Got

There are hundreds of different diet plans and pharmacies are well-stocked with appetite depressants and wonder drugs that make all kinds of promises but can seriously affect your health. The fact is that the human body itself is quite capable of achieving the goal you set for it and if you are unhappy with your weight, the big question to ask yourself is – What is the cause of my problem?

In most cases, excess poundage is very simply caused by the wrong eating and drinking habits. Some women develop a mental aberration that brings about an unhealthy desire for excessive indulgence. If food is being used as a habitual pacifier in your life or if you have an abnormal craving for fattening food or drink, you may need some form of counselling to help you discover the reason for this behaviour.

Sometimes a smart gal can figure out the problem without professional help. Often the magic solution to overeating or eating the wrong things can be challenged by changing your eating pattern.

Margaret lost ten unwanted pounds by – guess what – knitting. Let us explain. Margaret's excess weight came from nibbling while watching television.

"Excess poundage is caused by the wrong
eating and drinking habits..."

It seemed she couldn't just "sit there doing nothing". By occupying her hands with knitting needles she found this satisfied the need for activity.

Alice found a more startling solution. Living alone, she had fallen into the habit of reading her favourite Stephen King thrillers while she ate at the table. When she resolutely put reading as an AFTER meal activity she ate much less.

Maureen, who loved to dawdle over her meals, changed her habits. The meals she ate alone (breakfasts) were the ones she overate – hot cakes with syrup and butter, bacon, home fries. Now Maureen eats her breakfast from the kitchen windowsill, standing up.

Obesity is now regarded as a disease of epidemic proportions. Of the women now on "diets", ninety percent skip meals and thirty-three percent attempt "crash" diets and/or take over the counter appetite suppressants.

The majority will remain overweight because they are going about it in the wrong way. When an individual goes to extremes with a sudden low-cal or low-carb diet, that magnificently protective machine, the body, regards the sudden decrease in fuel as a sign of starvation and the metabolism slows down. The dieter loses energy and becomes less active, burning up fewer calories, as a result, and ends up at virtually the same weight as before. In other words "crash" diets can be self-defeating.

Women who exercise regularly have more muscle-mass than those who don't and those with more muscle tissue are more efficient calorie-burners and can lose weight faster. No diet can be truly successful without a good exercise programme to make it work. Remember, the human body is composed of lean mass (muscle, bone, vital tissue and organs) and fat mass, and the right exercise routine helps to decrease body fat and increase muscle mass.

Don't be a "wishful shrinker"; develop sensible eating habits and a regular exercise routine. Simple well-balanced meals that include small portions of fresh fruit, a high-fibre carbohydrate, vegetable or cereal, a protein food (egg, cottage cheese, skinless chicken or fish), and vegetables will provide you with all the nutrition you need. If you can stay off the fats, sauces, gravies, soups, salad dressings and desserts and reduce your intake of sugar and salt, you should experience steady weight loss and be able to keep it off without starving yourself. Follow the dieters Golden Rule: a satisfying breakfast, a light lunch and a lighter supper. If you stick to these sensible meals with no snacking in between, you will have your weight under control and be able to keep it that way through the happy years ahead.

Please remember that beverages such as herbal teas and the occasional glass of dry white wine can be enjoyed; but coffee is something to be taken sparingly since it can interfere with your natural ability to break down cholesterol and even contribute to weight gain, without you being aware of it. Soda water, though low in calories, is high in salt so it can put you in a no–win situation.

For your own health and well being, try to eat fresh foods rather than those from cans and packages. DO read labels so you can see what kind of ingredients you are putting into your precious body. Labelling rules

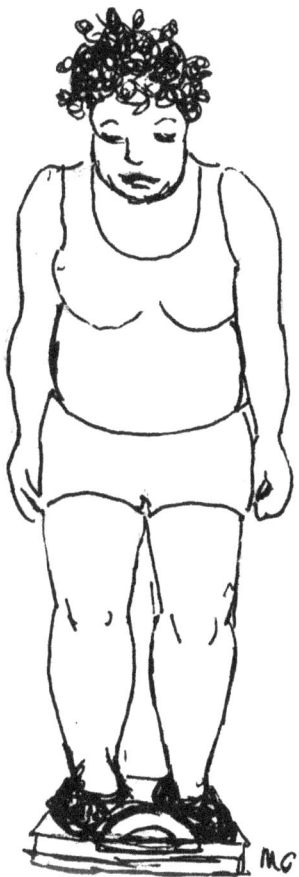

"Don't be a 'Wishful Shrinker'!"

call for ingredients to be listed in order of proportion. In other words, "orange" juice containing "water, sugar, citric acid, juice from orange concentrate" really isn't going to provide the amount of Vitamin C which occurs in pure orange juice.

Beware of excessive sugar, fat and salt and confine snacks to raw vegetables and fresh fruits only. We can borrow a word of advice from the ancient Greeks who established the theory of the Golden Mean which simply says that everything should be taken in moderation and nothing to excess. The slimmest and healthiest people we know subscribe to this philosophy.

Case History: Betty

Betty had a very unhappy marriage that ended in a violent quarrel followed by heated court battles. Her husband had constantly belittled her and pursued other women through their brief marriage.

After the divorce, Betty's life changed. She was a good cook and had always enjoyed fine food and wine. On her own she began to eat and drink excessively and her weight soared. She finally sought the help of a therapist who discovered that Betty was actually substituting food for sex and male companionship. Yet at the same time, by remaining overweight, she subconsciously made herself unattractive to men and this meant she could maintain a sheltered existence, free from having to face relationships that could cause her any further heartbreak. It was only when she was able to understand her emotional hang-ups that she was able to deal with her physical one.

TUNING UP THE ENGINE

If you have done little exercise or paid scant attention to body fitness over the years, don't despair. All you need is a sincere desire to emerge from your chrysalis and flutter forth towards that very desirable butterfly image we have in mind for you.

Here are three ways to exercise that cost nothing and can do you nothing but good:

- Put on the radio and stretch and swing and defy gravity as you do your household chores. Music has a stimulating effect on your entire body and mind. Begin and end the day with movement to music and you will feel happier for it.

- Take your dog for a long walk. Pets in their enthusiasm can make you walk further and at a brisker pace than if you were alone. (Our friend Josie, sweet and sixty, met and fell in love with a charming gentleman who exercised his poodle, Jim, in the same park she exercised her Great Dane, Marigold.)

- Walk briskly, with arms swinging. Breathe deeply and enjoy the sights and sounds around you. If you live near a beach, walking barefoot in sand can be a

"Take your dog for a walk"

MG.

"Making the most of every muscle
you've got"

wonderful exercise for the feet and leg muscles. Walk to work, to the shop, to see a friend, plan to walk a greater distance each time you go out.

MAKE LOVE

According to Dr. A. Friedman, sex is one of the most effective exercises. In his book "Sex Can Keep You Thin", Dr. Friedman even comes up with a formula to illustrate his theory: (Sn. x 200) + Sx.).

Sn. represents the number of snacks you don't eat because you'd rather make love and Sx. the number of times you make love. Naturally the more often you make love and the more active you are in the process, can determine just what benefit you can expect.

We can't think of any more exciting way to increase blood circulation and improve body condition. So get out those sexy negligees, ladies, and get on with this serious business of losing weight. Don't confine sex to the bedroom, check out the living room carpet, the patio chair, the deserted beach...anywhere in fact, that's out of public view and there won't be interruptions.

MAKING THE MOST OF EVERY MUSCLE YOU'VE GOT

There is an old saying: "What you don't use, you lose" and this holds true for both body and mind. The average woman does not use even a quarter of her mental and physical capacity, and as the years progress; she finds her body and mind less responsive than before. The muscles and cells first "go on holiday" and then into perpetual hibernation.

However "retired" you are, you should make a point of using as many parts of your body and brain as you can or you will find yourself getting weaker and weaker as the cells, bones and muscles steadily degenerate.

For those of you who like to exercise at home, we are including a few simple routines that use almost every part of the body. We have discovered that the most beneficial exercise session should begin with stretches; move on to include positions either lying or sitting on the floor, work up to a standing position and progressive movements across the floor and end in a horizontal or inverted position. If you end each set of exercises with deep breathing you won't feel tired.

Start the music and begin. . .

1. Chin, Arms and Midriff
a) Stretch arms above your head and reach one hand after the other towards the ceiling. Look upwards. Note: If you get used to lifting your chin while standing, sitting or walking, you will help prevent that extra fold from developing under your chin, a "double chin". Check your mirror and you can see what we mean.

b) While still in a stretched position, clasp hands, straighten arms and, with palms pressed against one another over your head, lean directly sideways without twisting the body. Slowly straighten up and repeat to the other side.

2. Tummy and Waist
a) Lie on the bed, legs straight and feet propped against the wall, with hands stretched above your head, pull tummy in as far as it will go and hold for 8 counts. Release and repeat 10 times.

b) Lying on your back with arms stretched outwards, bend your knees and roll lower body from side to side, keeping shoulders on the floor. Repeat at least 20 times.

3. Thighs and Hips
    Lie on your side with head supported by your hand, with elbow bent. Stretch legs straight and then swing them back and forth alternately for 8 counts. Straighten legs again and raise them both together, then lower to the floor. Repeat several times.

4. Legs and Bottom
a) Stand with both hands holding a railing or chair back. Without letting the upper body tip forward, raise one leg 6 inches off the floor behind you and bounce it up and down for 8 counts. Be sure to keep both legs straight throughout the exercise.

b) Lie face down on the floor, with elbows bent and head resting on your hands. Keeping your left leg straight, raise it about 6 inches off the floor and then lower. Repeat with other leg. Repeat 6 times.

5. Chest and Arms

a) Bend your elbows in front of you and lift them to the level of your bust. Grip hands together and pull them one against the other without lowering your elbows. Repeat for at least 8 counts.

b) Lift your elbows into the same position as No. 5a and press your fingertips together with the thumbs pointing towards the centre of your chest. Keeping the pressure on your fingertips, extend your arms outwards and then inwards towards your chest. Repeat 10 times.

RELAXATION AND DEEP BREATHING

Round the back and drop the upper body and arms forward. Completely relax in this position, blowing all the air in your lungs out through your mouth. Gradually unroll the body upwards, breathing in continuously through the nose until the body is in an upright position with hands stretched above your head and the lungs expanded to the fullest. Repeat 4 times. Note: It is wise to conclude every exercise session with a shoulder stand. An inverted position will return the blood and oxygen to your head and make you feel great.

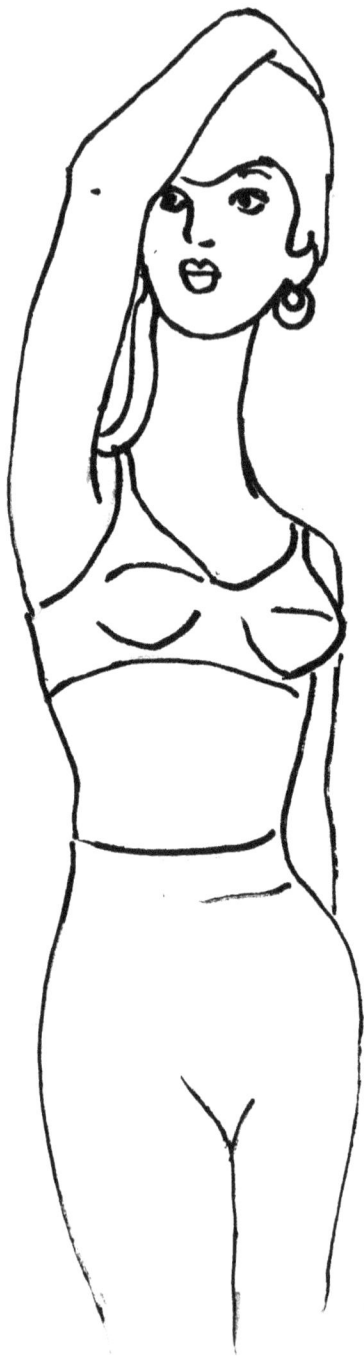

"Get support"

MORE ON MAKING THE MOST OF YOUR BODY

Dance, to us both, is the elixir of life; not only because it is fun but because it can tone every muscle in the body. Joining a gym, an aerobics class or a creative dance group is a positive step in the right direction towards putting your entire system to work. All types of dancing from salsa to meringue can leave you exhilarated, not just from the physical activity but for the opportunities for social contact.

Dance is a marvellous form of therapy for loneliness, depression and stress and can be enjoyed at any age.

However, if you have serious back or heart trouble, or have suffered any kind of debilitating injury or disease that precludes attempting heavy exercise, you may want to try water aerobics. We know a lady of ninety-one, partially crippled by a leg injury, who does one hundred movements in water every day to keep her muscles in shape; and at last report was steadily improving her ability to walk.

You have to regard exercise as a necessary tune-up for mind and body. Just as a car battery runs down and ultimately becomes useless from inactivity, so too do your own mechanisms. Fitness can be described as the condition that ensures that you can look, feel and do your best. Exercise enables you to deliver oxygen and nutrients to the tissues and removes waste through the pores in the form of perspiration. Physical fitness involves the peak performance of the heart, lungs and muscles of the body and helps to improve mental alertness and emotional stability.

Important tip! GET SUPPORT! Do wear a good support bra when you are working out. Physical activity can put a strain on breast muscles and tissues. Never, never exercise without wearing a bra. Support tights can give weak leg muscles and veins the help they need to keep you dancing or jogging without undue stress. Do wear them when working out. You will feel far more energetic and your body will thank you later.

Case History: Marie Blanchard

Marguerite will always remember Marie Blanchard, a blind student at the Arthur Murray Studio in Montreal. She celebrated her seventy-eighth birthday by competing for and attaining her Gold Medal, one of the highest standards of accomplishment for a ballroom dancer of any age. As Arthur Murray said "Anyone can learn to dance."

PRIVATE AND CONFIDENTIAL - EXERCISES FOR THE INNER YOU

Today, obstetricians often instruct new mothers on how to perform little exercises to keep the muscles that control the vagina strong. Whether or not you have had children, these exercises can't fail to help you. They are so easy and private that you could even perform some of them in public and nobody would be aware of this. Most women prefer to go through the routine in bed.

Learning how to tighten these muscles is a little like learning how to wiggle your ears. They are not as easy to control as the ones that move your legs and arms so you have to first learn how to make them respond. One way to practice is while you are urinating. Pee a bit, then stop. Repeat four times while your bladder is emptying. The next step is to do the same contractions while not urinating – and this does take a bit of practise. Once you have mastered the contractions, you can practise while waiting in the dentist's reception room or watching television. The more you practise the stronger the muscles will become.

Ready for step two? Lie in bed with your knees bent. Insert a squeaky-clean finger into your vagina. Contract the muscles and feel the tightening. See what we're getting at? Now gently think of pushing out and contracting in against your finger. Tighten and relax as many times as feels comfortable.

We don't need to tell you why these exercises make for better sex for both you and your partner. And here's an extra bonus: these exercises are an excellent way of toning up the muscles that hold things – like your bladder – in place. Women who have undergone surgery for prolapse of the bladder will find them particularly beneficial.

GILDING THE LILY

Nothing makes a woman feel happier and more confident than knowing that she looks attractive. In this chapter we talk about those final touches that will make you look your best.

Center Stage

For some reason, the world seems to feel that a woman should "dress her age", that automatically, at a certain age, she should abandon the latest creations and stick to dull, uninteresting styles and colours. We make no secret of the fact that we select some of our fun clothes from the junior department and revel in dramatic colours – and even enjoy some rather daring swim suits and tee shirts. We are still very careful in our selections because we both know our own limitations and so far we still draw compliments from the opposite sex. The secret is in knowing just how far you should go and understanding just where your weaknesses lie in regards to your shape.

Tailored clothing, simple styles that never go out of vogue, are the best investments; and co-ordinates that mix and match add variety to the wardrobe.

Don't be afraid to experiment with bright colours. The shades to be wary of are beige, grey and black. These tones can be aging since the mature face may not have enough radiance to balance these rather dour tones. If you do have such items in your wardrobe don't discard them, but do add some bright and lively accessories to warm them up

CHOOSING THE CLOTHES THAT ARE YOU

When you next shop, take along a knowledgeable friend and let her help choose something that flatters you rather than select an item which, while it may be trendy, does not enhance the good features of your face and figure. The ideal choice will cover up your

"Selecting the clothes that are you"

weak points and bring out your best. If an outfit doesn't excite you, leave it on the rack and put your money on something more stimulating.

Do buy attractive things to wear at home. Long flowing gowns or sexy pyjamas help you present a seductive picture. If you want to really wake up the male in your life remember that fire-engine red is the super attention-getter, the number one "turn-on" colour. You owe it to yourself to include one red negligee and one red cocktail gown in your wardrobe – with undies to match.

Oddly enough you will find that it doesn't really cost more to buy lounge wear that is foxy and flattering than to purchase dowdy dusters that have become associated with household drudges. If you have any left in your closet, throw them out. Put your pennies towards getting something seductive to wear at home. For some reason we tend to look our worst in front of the husband we take for granted until, one day, he walks out the door.

Remember, if YOU don't look good at home, he'll be looking good for someone outside – and you'll only have that old grey duster to blame!

If you're particularly well endowed, you might find it helpful to wear a soft support bra in bed to keep you looking good for your bed partner – he may just enjoy removing it himself when the mood gets hot.

We are not fans of heavy support in the form of girdles because these can restrict your blood flow. Please don't wear a girdle unless you feel it is absolutely necessary and then, please, try to manage with the lightest support you can. If you take our advice and work on building up your muscles you won't need extra support. The natural girdle of tummy muscles was meant to provide its own support. GET THESE MUSCLES IN SHAPE!

YOUR CROWNING GLORY

Earlier we touched lightly on hair problems – now we hope to give further suggestions for making the most of your crowning glory. Just as you visit your doctor or dentist for periodic check-ups, you should visit a professional hairdresser periodically for a good haircut and advice on hair colour, hair care etc.

One of the most terrible habits is wearing curlers in the street, at home and – worst of all – in bed. A head full of wire, sponge and plastic and a face covered in cream are big turnoffs for most men. After you have washed and set your hair, dry it in the fastest possible time and comb it out.

Other unflattering beauty regimes such as de-fuzzing, trimming nails and tweezing eyebrows should be done in private and as quickly as possible. Don't condemn your partner to these nightly performances!

By the way, just how do you get into bed with your man? Are you fresh and fragrant as you emerge from a bath or shower? If not, you may witness a "Disappearing Man Act" in the not too distant future.

Your scent lingers all night long, for better or worse. After your shower, a dusting of powder and a splash of cologne should make you a very desirable bed partner for the man in your life. (Remember, sex is the best exercise.)

Don't save perfumes and colognes for evenings out – use them to your advantage all day and all night.

PUTTING YOUR BEST FOOT FORWARD

As we get older, we tend to lean more towards comfort rather than style when shopping for footwear. The trick is to select shoes that offer both comfort and style. Lower heels can still be pretty and dainty if you choose a design that flatters your feet. Never buy shoes that don't really fit just because they happen to be on sale or happen to be the latest rage. You certainly can't put your best foot forward if you are in agony! If you have to stand all day long, try to change from one heel level to another during the day so the pressure does not remain on one section of your foot. Shop around and be prepared to pay a little more for shoes that offer both good looks and a comfortable fit.

FACE UP TO THE NEW YOU

Since every woman's face is different, we won't attempt to give you detailed advice on makeup and skin care. As we mentioned before, cosmetic advice is readily available from professional cosmetologists and numerous publications. In better cosmetic departments the staff is trained to give you honest and valuable advice on purchases. Avoid those who seem determined only to sell you their most expensive products; consult those who seem truly sympathetic to your own needs. What we would like to do is give you a few tips we have learned over the years:

MG.

"Face up to the new you"

1. After age forty you should refrain from using face powder entirely. Powder tends to cake and emphasize lines. Choose instead a liquid foundation that blends with your natural skin tone. Never choose one that is darker since this can bring out lines and shadows. A slight sheen gives your complexion a youthful glow. A heavy matte finish tends to make you look older.

2. Use a blush and blend it gently, high on your cheek bones, with a light touch on the tip of your nose, chin and forehead to add lively colour to your complexion.

3. Be careful not to overdo when applying eye shadows and eyeliners.

4. Select hypoallergenic, water-based mascara, and remove it with a clean cotton pad saturated with eye lotion.

5. Use a pencil lip liner or brush to outline the lips before filling in with colour. Avoid lipsticks or blushers that have blue or purple tones as these tend to be aging.

6. Don't be afraid to use bright lipsticks. Blot lip colour, apply more and then blot again for a more long-lasting effect.

Note: Always use a moisturizer with sunscreen under your liquid makeup if your skin is likely to be exposed to sunlight.

GIVE THE LADY A HAND...

Give your hands the same skin treatments you give your face. Avoid bright nail polish that can draw attention to your hands and blemishes, veins and other imperfections.

"Charm is a sort of bloom on a woman...
if you don't have it, it doesn't matter
what else you have"

Sir James Barne

Ready For Action

THE BUTTERFLY EMERGES

"Charm is a sort of bloom on a woman. If you have it, you don't need anything else, if you don't have it, it doesn't matter what else you have."

Sir James Barne

When all is said and done, you can be the youngest and most beautiful woman in the entire world and still fail to be popular and attractive. Yes, the most important factor in this whole scenario is YOU, the you that is hidden away inside that magnificent exterior. Think of the people around you, what makes you like or dislike them. Are they open and friendly, with a happy disposition, or sour and complaining? Where do you fit in? The fact is that you are liked or disliked by how you make THEM feel. A man likes to be with you because you please his senses and make him feel good, you are attractive to look at, you are pleasant, you compliment him, you are a good listener, you place him on a pedestal, you don't constantly complain, you have a sense of humour, you consider his feelings, you are energetic, you do exciting things, you keep up with the latest news, you're a good conversationalist – yes, he feels happy in your presence, he wants to see more of you – this is the beginning of something good!

A man feels unhappy in your company if you do not please his senses, you are a chronic complainer, you belittle him, you nag and tear him down, you show no interest in his problems, you are not a good listener, you have no sense of humour and your conversation is limited. Why should he stick around? Would you? Think about it – the very qualities you seek in a man are the same ones he will like in you. There are many beautiful women who close the door on relationships simply because they lack interest in other people. Remember the old joke: the self-absorbed gentleman who, after talking about himself for more than an hour, said to his lady, "But enough about me, let's talk about you, what do you think about me?"

Remember, too, that your smile is your best facelift! No amount of money spent on surgery will make you attractive if your personality and disposition are not in tune. At best, artificial rejuvenation efforts are temporary. Underneath the exterior, the real "you" remains.

Your voice is important because it represents you in communication with others. Try to keep it at a pleasant level, it is never necessary to shout or nag. If you lower your voice, others will lower theirs. If you are shy about speaking out, improve your use of grammar and pronunciation by reading aloud to yourself. Put lively animation into your voice. Avoid slang phrases and, of course, foul or abusive language. Perhaps you would enjoy using a tape recorder to monitor your voice so that it sounds pleasant and unaffected. And always smile while on the phone – the smile will echo in your voice.

Once you start to give of yourself, you will receive. A woman is never old as long as she can look forward with eager anticipation to each new day and each new encounter, planning to make each day a little better than the one before, not just for herself but for those around her. If she can make each person who enters her life happier than they were before they met her, she will have acquired that most important attribute of all – CHARM. Try to be natural and unaffected with other people. Forget yourself and concentrate on making them feel good all over.

Remember, you are only old when:

Everything is wrong.
Everything is too much trouble.
Your glass is half empty – not half full.
You expect the worst of every new situation.
You are suspicious of new encounters.
You use age as an excuse.
You don't do the most with what you've got.

WHY GET OLD? AGE IS A STATE OF MIND

Case History: Ethlyn

Ethlyn, aged ninety-six, lives in a modest guest house in Ocho Rios. As she sips her morning coffee she chats with the cook, (whose children's names and ages she remembers) and with the gardener (to enquire after his mother's arthritis). She feeds, from the table, the birds that have gathered and smiles at the school children passing. She has friends of all ages: the delivery boy whom she taught to play bridge, the schoolchildren who seek help with their Math, and a charming gentleman who shares her memories of times passed. We once asked Ethlyn: "With such a wonderful life, do you have any unanswered prayers?" Ethlyn smiled and murmured, "Ah, to be seventy again!"

Falling in Love Again

So here you are, beautiful and happy with life and yourself, ready for love. You have dispelled the foolish fears, cast out the guilt which held you prisoner, assessed your good points and learned to live with what is less than perfect. So where do you find the ideal partner to explore this exciting new life before you? Well, we have some suggestions...

FALLING IN LOVE WITH THE MOST AVAILABLE MAN

So you are sixty or seventy and sexy, you've seen enough of other people's mistakes to understand, forgive and forget. You are perfect as you have learned how to look and feel your best, glowing with a new zest for life and, as the old song puts it, "nothing is missing but the man".

Well now, have you ever thought of falling in love with your husband? Think of the convenience! No need for excuses! No uncomfortable motel rooms! No whispered telephone calls! He's right there – available!

Of course you love your husband – paunch, falling hair and all – but are you "in love" with him? Do you look anxiously at the clock as his home-coming nears?

"Falling in love with your husband"

"Don't be ridiculous!" you may say. "We're not teenagers anymore!" But wouldn't it be fun to turn back the clock?

But Joe? Old Joe? As comfortable as an old bedroom slipper?

Take a look at old Joe there. Now think of the men belonging to your friends. How does Joe stack up? He must have something going for him if you've stuck with him all these years. If the flame is completely dead, you might consider looking for somebody else, but don't be too hasty.

Ask yourself: "If I died tomorrow, would another woman want Joe?"

You bet your sweet patootie!

Maybe old Joe doesn't look like Richard Gere or Denzel Washington – but could that paunch of his be partly your fault? Are you encouraging him to eat tasty low-calorie meals and inviting him to join you when you jog?

Stop thinking about what's wrong with old Joe. Start thinking of what's right with him – relive the memories you share, the good times and the bad times. You've survived both and this means a lot. And Joe has lived as long or longer than you have – he must have picked up some wit and wisdom along the way.

So here you are with this treasure waiting to be rediscovered. How do you go about it?

Show a little more affection. Compliment him. Join him in activities he enjoys and invite him to share your interests. Pinch the budget and take HIM out to dinner in a romantic setting. Go dancing. Drink wine.

How lucky you are to be a mature woman at this time. You have learned how to keep in perfect shape – or as perfect as Nature intended.

Science keeps you healthy.

Makeup keeps you pretty.

Exercise keeps you fit.

Common sense keeps your best foot forward.

You sensibly make use of all aids to rejuvenation – and Joe begins to realize that his little woman isn't the little woman she used to be. He may react by becoming:

Suspicious.

Pugnacious.

Confused.

He may take to phoning you at odd hours during the day. He may complain "You're never here anymore – what happened to you?" He may watch you leave for the new job or the new study course you're taking with a pitiful but brave – "Don't worry dear, I'll be alright by myself," (read deserted, unloved) – but if Joe is smart he will realize that for him every middle-aged man's dream has come true – a wonderful ultra-sexy woman, all his, with some new tricks that are going to blow his mind; and the best part – it's legal!

So the two of you have the whole house to make whoopee, as you begin a new courtship that will drive you both completely wild!

You think it can't happen? Read on!

Case History: Julia

It was a normal marriage with its ups and downs, like when Winston took up with his secretary and Julia went home to Mandeville. But she came back (what else could she do, she reasoned) and life – if not wildly exciting continued. Once-a-week Winston would say, "Feeling good, sweetheart?" And if Julia answered "Okay, darling", there would be a tussle between the sheets and sometimes Julia would have an orgasm. If her answer was "I'm a bit tired, sweetheart", Winston would roll over and go to sleep because it wasn't all that important.

Julia accepted that this was how a marriage was supposed to go – then something terrible happened to Julia on a crowded bus. She was standing and heard a woman whisper, "Junior, you get up and give your seat to that old lady."

The "old lady" was Julia!

Julia had never thought of herself as old – maybe mature, like Angelica Houston – but when she went home, she stripped and stood in front of her full-length mirror – and it was true!

She had looked at that same face for sixty-three years. Nothing wrong, basically, but some flab under the chin and more salt than pepper in the hair. Julia's eyes moved downward.

"Hello, body," she whispered, "where have you been all these years? You've lost your waistline, your boobs sag, you've turned me into – an old lady."

Julia went to work. She went to a lingerie sales-person she trusted and bought new brassieres. She joined an aerobics class and splurged on a new hairdo. She threw out the old cosmetics lurking sadly in her drawer and chose some really good new ones.

Next, Julia bought some bright new scarves to highlight the nicer items in her wardrobe, and sent the few dowdy items to a home for REAL old ladies. She bought a sex manual and read it.

Cut to Julia, three months later. She has certainly changed. She's a bit slimmer and a whole lot firmer. The new hairdo is brightened by a tint.

Winston notices it – tells himself, "Julia is blossoming out!" He listens to her now.

Winston knows he's on to a good thing. But let's be honest. Winston is pushing sixty-nine, and sometimes it isn't a case of Mr. Eveready, so Julia takes it nice and slow and easy – and things begin to happen. Winston discovers in Julia's cries of delight proof of his masterful manhood.

Their friends, noticing the secret grins Julia and Winston exchange, ask, "What's happened to these people?"

Nothing happened. They're just in love.

But suppose there is no Joe in your life? Simply because women tend to live longer than men, women are more often left alone in later years. But "alone" needn't mean "lonely". Consider...

FALLING IN LOVE WITH A YOUNGER MAN

It can happen without warning. He is the charming young man in your adult education class who joins you for the coffee break. He is the young salesman who sold you your car and drops by to see if you really understand how the fuel pump works. He is on your committee to raise funds for the day-care centre and sits with you as the day darkens to discuss the proceeds of the tag day sale – and who talks of his own dreams as you prove such a good listener. He's the shy young man in the library who walks you home. "What a nice young man!" you say to yourself as the friendship deepens – and then you notice something strange; your day begins when you see him, his sudden smile makes your head spin. You begin to read romantic poetry – and discover it finally makes sense . . . you are in love.

But, you tell yourself, you are old enough to be his mother – are you in your second childhood as every-body warned? But then . . . you are having a late drink after a business meeting, and he asks you to dance. As his body touches yours, your sense quickens and you feel his physical response.

How could it have happened? There is nothing odd in your feeling love for him but by what miracle could

"Falling in love with a younger man"

he love you? Don't ask, lady – accept this miracle. If you have the courage – it is certainly worth it. Love between an older woman and a younger man – read Colette's sensuous stories of love between a courtesan and a boy half her age – can be very special, a delight shared by all too few.

So how to proceed? No need to compete with sweet sixteen in bikini or tennis shorts; just be the best you possible. The older woman can offer pure romance; she can lounge in a filmy cover-up beside the tennis court, with his favourite drink waiting, as he emerges from the game with the sweaty, dishevelled young woman who has beaten him twenty-love. An older woman can offer pure romance with no strings. She allows him to stretch his wings, confide his secret thoughts in a way he never could with the girl next door. She is undoubtedly a better listener, having had years of practice, and most of all she asks no promises and seeks no commitments. She appreciates him, under-stands him, and laughs with him but not at him.

But how long can such a love last? Forever? It does happen, but chances are there will come a time when you sense that this romance will end. So when do you say goodbye – just before it might occur to him to do so.

So was it worth it? Indeed it was!

But stop a bit – young romantic men are in short supply! True enough. So why not consider...

FALLING IN LOVE WITH A MAN YOUR OWN AGE

There is one paramount problem about falling in love with a man your own age – most of the good ones are already taken. What is more, statistics tell us that there is always a smaller number of widowers than of widows. This obviously narrows down the options.

A divorced man should be carefully studied before you become involved. Maybe his ex-wife knows something you ought to know.

A man who has remained unmarried into his fifties and sixties might be a true *Mummy's Boy* who never grows up and expects his woman to wash his dirty socks and dose him with cough syrup when he spends a night with her. A man who has never married may be a man no woman ever wanted. An unmarried middle-aged man may have a close gentleman friend who shares his flat and whips up delightful little omelettes. (Such men are usually excellent friends, however, if you need a shoulder to cry on.)

A bachelor is often proud of the fact that he can cook. A word of warning: this is not necessarily the advantage you think. Why? A man is incapable of buying one sweet pepper. A man doesn't cook for the two of you – he cooks for the Reggae Boyz. As a result, his refrigerator is full of leftovers and generally, men who cook usually have very fat dogs. A man is hypnotised by strange recipes. Once you and he are a couple; he is quite likely to stride from the refrigerator demanding, "Why haven't we got any black olives or canned clams?" Obviously because some woman has been squandering money on milk and rice.

A widower who speaks fondly of his late spouse is frequently a fine love object. Since his marriage was a happy one he is probably a joy to live with. Besides all this, he knows that women often put rollers in their hair and muck on their faces, and that they sometimes sweat, and so he will accept any number of things a normal woman does. A man your own age also shares your frame of reference. When you tell him your Uncle Bob died in the war he knows you mean the one in Vietnam and not the one in Iraq and he grew up with Sinatra, not Beenie Man. Shared tastes can make for cosy intimacy with this man who prefers a grown-up woman to a teenager and fine wine to a soda.

Over sixty years, however, men develop little ways that may seem peculiar to other people. A wife of many years is exposed to these gradually, but if you come up against a new set of habits, full blown, it can be unnerving. (Of course you have your own little peculiarities but that's HIS problem.)

Whatever a man is in his youth he will be more so as he ages. A cautious youth will become a paranoid old man insisting when he misplaces something, that somebody has stolen it. A careless youth will become an old man who forgets to post letters or zip his fly. Only a most unusual (and desirable) man will change his religion or his politics after fifty: the few who do are worth cultivating because they have open minds. Most older men hoard things, filling desk drawers, kitchen cupboards and their garages with worthless memorabilia. You can understand keeping old cheque stubs, school yearbooks, or photographs of himself as a kid, but some older men have been known to squirrel away such valuables as old supermarket cash register slips, envelopes addressed to "Occupant" and every copy of Popular Mechanics ever printed.

Anything electronic attracts middle-aged men who hoard weird and wonderful bits of equipment which they are sure to find useful whenever February 29 falls on a snowy Friday. Some of the things older men save are ten-year-old credit bills long paid, broken bits of pipe, parts of machines that don't work anymore, empty pill bottles, old Crazy Glue tubes, and anything else that might come in handy some day.

A woman who gets the "hots" for a lovable contemporary may find passion pales if she has to hunt for him behind piles of old newspapers. There is nothing you can do about this. If you throw anything away he will know and it will be something he was going to use first thing tomorrow morning.

Live and let live, however, is the way to go. And here is the good news: many a man who appears to be set in his ways is secretly an adventurer at heart, eager for new experiences. For him, a woman his own age who understands him, a mature woman with new ideas can be just what the doctor ordered.

Enjoy! But take warning...

FALLING IN LOVE WITH AN OLDER MAN

There are three reasons for falling in love with an old man, that is, a man who looks old and acts old. There are, please note, some young kids over seventy who have a twinkle in their eye, youth in their hearts and all other equipment in working order. Latch on to one of these, ladies.

But what about 'OLD OLD' men? There are three reasons this might be a choice.

Reason No. 1: You've always wanted to be a geriatric nurse.

Reason No. 2: A giant meteor has landed and killed all other men on earth.

Reason No.3: He is terribly rich.

Serious Options

Readers who have stayed with us up to now may feel we're being a bit superficial in our approach. It's all very well to talk of beginning a new love life after your first half-century, but, we know as well as you do that it isn't always easy. The loss of a beloved mate of many years is a traumatic experience. What happens when hubby leaves a helpmate of many years for a trophy wife? If a widow is fortunate, she has enough financial security so that she doesn't have to drastically change her lifestyle. But what does a woman do, in later years, if she is caught in the treadmill of an unsatisfactory marriage? What does she do if the relationship shatters? She knows some action must be taken but too often the question is "what" and "what with".

DOING THE MOST WITH THE RESOURCES YOU'VE GOT

If a woman looks forward to meagre or scanty alimony payments, or a modest life insurance policy, or if she has managed to secure a small nest egg, she is faced with the task of developing a plan of action to increase potential worth with sane and sensible investments that can pay a substantial interest rate. At the same time, she should be seeking ways to raise investment capital by using God-given talents and "making the most of what she's got".

It is comforting to note that recent statistics indicate that many of the world's most famous persons did not achieve notability or financial success until they were well over sixty years old. So your best, and perhaps most lucrative years are yet to come.

Regard making and managing money successfully as a new and interesting hobby and see how far you can take it with reliable professional help. The first thing to do is look at your assets, take stock of your bank balances, vehicle and property titles and your annuities. Where do you really stand? If you are on your own, mortgage paid up and children grown with families of their own, you may wish to sell the family home and downsize to a town house or efficiency apartment. This move would give you not only more freedom but should provide you with a reasonable amount of money to invest wisely – perhaps even enough capital so that you could live off the interest.

If your house is paid for and you don't want to sell, you could use it as collateral for a loan or re-mortgage. YOUR HEIRS THEN COULD PICK UP THE MORTGAGE AND SELL THE HOUSE AND NO ONE WOULD BE THE LOSER – CERTAINLY NOT YOU!

Many older persons have accumulated paintings or family objects d'arte which have become antiques. You may want to get these evaluated and consider putting them up for auction by a reputable dealer. Income from this can help you raise your ante on the investment market.

Clutter and general bric-a-brac can also bring a few dollars. Everything from old pots and picture frames, stamp collections and odd dishes, has their value and can attract buyers. Just declare a garage sale or flea market for a day and collect the cash.

What about your own talents? If you are employed and enjoying pleasant, lucrative work, no doubt you will continue. If not, have you considered marketing your own talents? Are you good at the computer, playing the piano, sewing or painting? What about offering your services as a private tutor? Could you consider starting a small catering service? Do you love to garden? Why not grow plants and seedlings for sale? Do you know a garden shop which might be interested? Ideas come from the most unusual sources. One enterprising senior purchased everyday cleaning items in bulk five gallon containers and divided them into smaller bottles for sale to neighbours. She gives them a good price they save storage space and she makes money – a winning combination.

Have you ever thought of becoming a business tycoon? Don't laugh – consider Nicola...

Case History: Nicola

Nicola, a free lance journalist, suddenly became a widow at fifty-four. Her husband, David, had operated a small factory – "Don't worry your pretty little head about such things," David used to say. After he died she discovered that the business was (gulp!) one million dollars in debt – and had no further borrowing power. What's more, David's personal bank account was in overdraft and he had not settled his personal taxes.

Since she was co-owner of the matrimonial home and the house was paid for she did not acknowledge or probate the Will. As sole heir and only living Director of the company she saw it was up to her to take charge of the business.

Nicola formed a new Board of Directors and began examining liabilities with a view to turning them into assets. She immediately began down-sizing the business, selling surplus equipment to clear the debt and producing only the best-selling products.

So where did this journalist learn to bring a business out of the red? She sought professional advice – from lawyers and accountants. She put new plans into action; revamped the staff hierarchy, collected outstanding debts and re-planned company policy and procedure. In three months the company was out of debt and remained that way until she sold it, eight years later, as a successful business. She then invested the money and moved into comfortable retirement.

BEWARE OF SCAMS, LOAN SHARKS AND GET-RICH-QUICK SCHEMES!!!

We can't stress how important it is to invest in and deal with only recognized and licensed banks, building societies and other recommended financial institutions that are government regulated.

Remember:

Rule One: Recognize your weaknesses and seek to turn them into strengths, and to turn your liabilities into assets.

Rule Two: Make a clear list of all your assets and make a plan on how to move forward. Don't be afraid to ask questions of legal and financial professionals. They are there to serve you.

Case History: Verna

After nearly 35 years of back-breaking work in a London hospital, Verna, a Jamaican nurse, returned to Jamaica to join her sister, Myrna, at the family home in Port Antonio.

Verna brought her life savings in British pounds, which, when translated into Jamaican money, left her reasonably secure for her retirement.

One day she was in the bank when she saw a debonair gentleman in a dapper dark suit and tie, staring at her.

"Haven't I met you somewhere before?" asked the man, "Perhaps London, or Paris?" He introduced himself as "Richard Smith, attorney–at–law".

A conversation ensued and he offered to carry her packages home to her house on East Palm Avenue. She invited him in for tea and they found they had a lot in common. He was cer- tainly a well-travelled man.

A few days later, he dropped in again. This time he told her excitedly that he had just purchased some land to do an upscale housing development and he would like her to see it. He explained that he intended to triple his money in two years and he invited her to buy into the project.

He hired a taxi and took her to view the scenic property, perched high on a hill, overlooking Port Antonio, and he showed her some plans that he was "trying to get approved", BUT he "urgently needed" one million Jamaican dollars in cash. He would pay her back with "substan- tial interest" in three months, if she could help him with the money to launch the project.

Verna thought the deal sounded fine and did not even think to tell Myrna about it.

The following day she accompanied Richard to the bank and transferred the money to him. He, in turn, gave her an official-looking receipt signed "Richard Smith".

Then, "Richard" disappeared.

After several weeks with no word from "Richard", a worried Verna went to the Port Antonio Police, who told her, quite plainly, that she had lost her money to a con artist known as Johnnie McQuick, a lawyer, indeed, but one that had been disbarred for many years from his profession for fraudulent dealings, and had a history of convictions that ranged from credit card scams to selling false lottery tickets.

"We'll add your name to the list of complainants but finding him won't be easy," warned a big burley policeman, "and in any event, it is quite unlikely you will get your money back."

Placed in a properly regulated 5-year ,tax-free investment account, Verna's one million dollars could have earned up to 12.5% compounded tax-free interest on a 3-month roll-over, which could have secured her a steady income for future retirement years.
Verna felt so foolish, she just sat down and cried.

And Now Before We Go

DIFFERENT STROKES

Love is the world's best medicine. We hope you take large doses regularly. Love brings a sparkle to the eye, a lilt to the walk, and a wonderful feeling that all's right with the world – despite the newspaper headlines and the unfriendly way we treat this earth we live on. Yes, love is as exciting at sixty as at sixteen – maybe it's even better, given the polish of wisdom and the common sense of maturity. Maybe there isn't a new man in your life – maybe you don't particularly want one right now! But you do need love!

FALLING IN LOVE WITH EVERYBODY

We're not suggesting promiscuity – you know us better than that by now – but this book carries no money back guarantee of a prince on a white horse riding out of the sunset. Even if you followed all of our suggestions, even if you've managed to wipe the cobwebs from your mind regarding romance, love and sex (and added some magic of your own) please don't wait for that Glass Slipper!

All of us want to live our lives to the fullest but it does not follow that this can only be achieved with a man. Some older women may feel that true freedom means freedom from hair dye, lipstick, and slinky negligees. They may feel that their new freedom means freedom to pursue a new profession, a favourite sport, or to "fall in love" with a cause or a community.

A truly happy woman, whether she has a special man to love or not, DOES fall in love with everybody. Her overtures win smiles from others in response, and she finds that people who were strangers are interesting people like herself, with their joys and sorrows, wit and wisdom. We are all part of the human race but as some of us get older we make the mistake of resigning from the World's Biggest Club. We go through the same old conversations with the same old people until they, like ourselves, are bored to tears.

Sometimes we become almost paranoid: somebody, possibly of another race, religion or income bracket, is out to "get" us. We begin to be sure the younger generation is going to the dogs and everybody under sixty is empty-headed. This is particularly annoying since people refuse to talk loud enough to be properly heard and young kids just out of school are managing banks, becoming surgeons, running countries.

Meet our friend June . . .

Case History: June

At sixty-seven, June had a list of people who made her uneasy: Billy, the neighbours' son, she considered delinquent; Mrs. Johnson, the doctor's wife was much too flashy; the high school principal, whom she suspected of being Hispanic, seemed to have a lot of crazy ideas.

June complained of strange aches and pains. It was hard to go to sleep at night. Her stomach "acted up" frequently.

June's doctor had no medicine to cure June's strange ailments. Instead of reaching for his prescription pad he looked her straight in the eye and gave her this "medical advice": "Make an effort to get to know these terrible people who frighten you."

June was not a fool. Her doctor had got her through three babies, family chicken pox, measles and flu, so she figured it was worth a try...

Let June tell her story:

"I invited young Billy over for biscuits and lemonade, and you know he's not a bad kid, a bit extreme but then so was Michael Manley. He's having a bit of trouble with Maths, but you know that was my best subject and I'm helping him with his homework.

"I dropped in on Mrs. Johnson, the doctor's wife, to take her some of my guava jelly, and she gave me an interesting book to read about Ecology.

Nellie – that's Mrs. Johnson – invited me to go to this group fighting to clean up the river bed and you wouldn't believe what – don't get me started!

"Anyway, talking to Billy made me decide I didn't know much about school curriculum nowadays so I went to the PTA meeting and you know what, Mr. Garcia – he's the principal – is introducing a class on family relationships and he asked me to be a counsellor – it's really fun."

June was wearing a bright pink scarf which did wonders for her grey knit. Her cheeks were pinker, too. She gave us both a big hug. "Look," she said, "I don't want to kick you both out but Tony – that's Mr. Garcia – is coming by to discuss the counselling programme."

We passed him on the walkway – a nice-looking grey-haired guy, carrying a bunch of flowers...

By opening her heart, June had fallen in love with everybody. Was it so strange that somebody seemed to be falling in love with her?

FINDING YOUR OWN LIFESTYLE

What's perfect for me might not be perfect for you, and both of us must discover the lifestyle which makes us happiest.

Ellen, married to a beloved husband suffering from Alzheimer's, remains faithful – caring for him with love. She has enough love left over to work with retarded children.

Louise, at seventy, shares her charming flat with a gay gentleman and they entertain "almost like sisters!"

Norma, who manages a profitable computer store, has a Lesbian lover. Josie says sex has vanished from her marriage to Lou but now, in their seventies, they enjoy camping trips together. Perhaps one of the most interesting couples is that of Marni and Paul. Paul, an entrepreneur who has made more than a fortune, married Marni when she was a top model. They have lived through a tumultuous marriage, a civilized divorce, and lived apart for a decade. Now they share a seafront villa in Barbados. Paul has his side of the house – Marni has hers. They meet at four each day for tea on the veranda overlooking the beach. They are an utterly charming couple.

So what's the bottom line?

Be yourself! Your best possible self! Create yourself in your own image. You must be true only to yourself – the years ahead are YOUR years – don't take too seriously advice offered by others – including us – without careful thought – be an innovator, not an imitator.

AS FOR US –

God made us in two sexes – for excellent reasons. Women must decide for themselves when – and if – a physical relationship is necessary. The decision will vary according to each woman. As for us – we feel God knew what he was doing when he created male and female – and we intend to carry out His good design as long as we can.

POSTSCRIPT – THE SECRET IS OUT

There is no such thing as an "old woman"; there are just women who have mistaken the end of the second act for the final curtain. You, who read these words, are of another breed. You have spent the first half of your lives growing up, caring for others, accumulating the knowledge for living and loving. Now you are yourself again – possibly cast in an entirely new role,

The years after fifty – the fifties, sixties, seventies, eighties – offer a new beginning. These are the years you've been waiting for. Now, as your own woman, you are ready to take on the world – and ready for a new romance. All it takes is a plan and a streak of determination.

Practise the suggestions you have read in this book. Refuse to stay home alone. Renew old friendships and make new ones. Join a club, lobby for cleaner oceans, buy a bright red dress.

Brush up an old skill or learn a new one. Attend a yoga class. Teach needy kids. Travel to another town. Study a new language. Look at everybody – especially your nearest and dearest – as if seeing them for the first time. Discover all the wonders of human relationships.

Tint your hair. Choose a book with your eyes closed and read it to the finish, even if it is a saga of boatbuilding in ancient Egypt.

Visit a REAL old lady, take her flowers. Sing in the shower. Adopt a puppy. Nibble on carrots, smile at an unknown man. Do the most with what you've got.

This is YOU – YOUR time, YOUR best years. And if you are ready, this is the time for a new love. Step forward with confidence.

There is a new world to explore – even a lonely man out there (maybe closer than you think) waiting for a wonderful woman – a woman just like you.

The End

A Special Friendship

One night in the 1960s, two women met for the first time. The event was a fashion show in the famous old Myrtle Bank Hotel – now long gone – on the harbour front in Kingston, Jamaica.

Both women were journalists, both dancers. Marguerite was one of Jamaica's best known models; Cynthia had won an award for contributing to Jamaica's fashion industry. It was a friendship that was to last more than forty years.

Marguerite was born of British parents in Kingston, where she attended St. Andrew High School for Girls. Since 1975, she has lived in the heart of a lush, tropical rainforest, overlooking the blue Caribbean at San San in the north-eastern corner of Jamaica; while Cynthia, surrounded by surfing grand-children, lives by the sea across the island on the south coast. Both are active media workers.

Since Marguerite's first tap, ballroom and ballet lessons as a child, and seven years as a Gold Medal instructor in ballroom and dance sport at Arthur Murray studios in Montreal and Bermuda, exercise and healthy living have been a way of life for her. She continued to pursue careers in modelling, dance – sport, journalism, radio and television news presentation and her first love – painting – which she studied at the University of Guadalahara in Mexico. In 1988, she founded the Portland Environment Protection Association, recognized world wide as the role model for Latin America and the Caribbean. She has travelled extensively, interacting with government leaders and environmental groups through North America and Latin America.

Following the untimely death of her French-Canadian husband Claude, in 1995, she has proven herself a businesswoman, taking over a debt-ridden factory and turning it into a successful business. For her work as a writer, fashion model, news correspondent, artist, dancer and influence in environmental protection, she has been honoured by a number of organizations. These include the Fashion Academy Award "for out-standing service to Jamaica's fashion industry", Rotary International (Paul Harris Fellowship) "for furtherance of better understanding and friendly relations among the peoples of the world", the Institute of Jamaica bronze medal for Science "for environmental education", the Government of Jamaica Prime Minister's Medal of Appreciation (2003) "for service to Jamaica" (environmental preservation) and the Press Association of Jamaica Award "for outstanding service in the field of journalism (2003).

As a broadcaster, Marguerite continues to speak to an estimated 80,000 people before breakfast, two mornings per week, and holds twice-weekly Dancercise classes for "youngsters" over sixty-five, a group she calls the "Energizer Bunnies" because they keep going, and going, and going . . And her stated commitment is to get younger and healthier each year.

Cynthia, too, began life as a dancer, teaching tap in her home town of Stratford, Ontario. Writing, too, was an obsession – her first article, bought and paid for, appeared in The World Digest in 1938. From then she went on to teach modern dance in Toronto, and to write and edit for trade journals. Married to a fellow journalist of Jamaican parentage, Cynthia came with her husband to Jamaica in 1961 for a one month holiday. Both were immediately offered posts on a progressive weekly newspaper, and have remained until this day.

Like Marguerite, Cynthia has won recognition as a journalist. She was awarded the Silver Musgrave Medal from the Institute of Jamaica, and honorary Life Membership in the Press Association of Jamaica. Following a successful career writing dramas and documentaries for Canadian and British radio, she turned to film-making in the late 1960s. She has won awards for documentaries in the Jamaica Film Festival, and other regional festivals and was given the Jamaican film-makers Doctor Bird Award for excellence in that field. She has also been awarded for travel writing. Today she is recognized as one of Jamaica's best known writer-director of film documentaries, and now in her eighties, she is busily at work on three new video documentaries. Presently she is completing her first fiction book – a "whodunit" set in Jamaica.

Hobbies? Relaxing with fifteen grandchildren and seven great-grandchildren and snorkelling on the rapidly disappearing reef outside her window. Needless to say, like Marguerite she is an ardent environmentalist.

About The Authors

Cynthia Wilmot is recognized as one of Jamaica's best known writer/director of film documentaries, as well as an accomplished journalist. She was once awarded the Silver Musgrave Medal from the Institute of Jamaica and an Honorary Life Membership in the Press Association of Jamaica. Now in her eighties, she is busily at work on three new video documentaries and completing her first fiction book – a "whodunit" – set in Jamaica. She is a true testament to the idea that life begins after fifty.

Marguerite Gauron, like Cynthia, is a talented journalist. She has received the Jamaica Press Association's award for outstanding service in the field of journalism, along with numerous accolades for her work as a writer, fashion model, news correspondent, artist, dancer and environmentalist. Known as the 'Voice of Portland', Marguerite continues to speak to an estimated 80,000 people before breakfast two mornings per week.